CHILE

in Pictures

Francesca Davis DiPiazza

TF
CB
Twenty-First Century Books

Contents

Lerner Publishing Group realizes that current information and statistics quickly become out of date. To extend the usefulness of the Visual Geography Series, we developed www.vgsbooks.com, a website offering links to up-to-date information, as well as in-depth material, on a wide variety of subjects. All of the websites listed on www.vgsbooks.com have been carefully selected by researchers at Lerner Publishing Group. However, Lerner Publishing Group is not responsible for the accuracy or suitability of the material on any website other than www.lernerbooks.com. It is recommended that students using the Internet be supervised by a parent or teacher. Links on www.vgsbooks.com will be regularly reviewed and updated as needed.

INTRODUCTION — 4

THE LAND — 8

▶ Boundaries. The North. The Central Valley. The Southern Zone. Mountains. Bodies of Water. Climate. Flora and Fauna. Natural Resources and Environmental Issues. Cities.

HISTORY AND GOVERNMENT — 20

▶ The Conquest. Spanish Rule. Independence. Bernardo O'Higgins Riquelme. Years of Development. Internal Tensions. The War of the Pacific and Nitrates. Economic Decline and Presidential Power. Political Disunity. Salvador Allende Gossens. Pinochet and Military Rule. Return to Democracy. The Twenty-First Century. Government.

THE PEOPLE — 38

▶ Population Distribution. Ethnic Groups. Education. Health. Ways of Life.

Website address: www.lernerbooks.com

Twenty-First Century Books
A division of Lerner Publishing Group
241 First Avenue North
Minneapolis, MN 55401 U.S.A.

VGS

web enhanced @ www.vgsbooks.com

CULTURAL LIFE   46

► Religion and Holidays. The Arts. Literature. Film.
Music. Sports and Recreation. Food.

THE ECONOMY   56

► Service Sector and Tourism. Industry, Mining,
and Manufacturing. Agriculture, Fishing, and
Forestry. Free Trade. Energy, Transportation,
and Communication. The Future.

FOR MORE INFORMATION

► Timeline   66
► Fast Facts   68
► Currency   68
► Flag   69
► National Anthem   69
► Famous People   70
► Sights to See   72
► Glossary   73
► Selected Bibliography   74
► Further Reading and Websites   76
► Index   78

Library of Congress Cataloging-in-Publication Data

DiPiazza, Francesca, 1961–
    Chile in pictures / by Francesca Davis DiPiazza.
        p.   cm. — (Visual geography series)
    Includes bibliographical references and index.
    ISBN-13: 978-0-8225-6587-1 (lib. bdg. : alk. paper)
    ISBN-10: 0-8225-6587-0 (lib. bdg. : alk. paper)
    1. Chile—Pictorial works. 2. Chile—Juvenile literature. I. Title.
F3065.057 2007
983—dc22   2006018879

Manufactured in the United States of America
1 2 3 4 5 6 – BP – 12 11 10 09 08 07

INTRODUCTION

Chileans sometimes say that when God was almost done making South America, he used all the leftover bits and pieces to make their country. And indeed, Chile does include almost all of Earth's possible landscape features. It has everything from desert, volcanoes, and ocean coast to rain forests, mountain streams, and islands.

Chile was a Spanish colony from the time of the founding of its capital city, Santiago, in 1541 until its independence in 1818. Native peoples resisted the Spanish conquest, but European weapons or illnesses overcame many of them. Some, however, retreated to the edges of the nation. Geographically isolated by the Andes Mountains to the east and the Pacific Ocean to the west, Chile developed with little interference from Spain. A wealthy group of Chilean landowners, mine owners, and the officials of the Roman Catholic Church dominated society and politics. The masses of mostly uneducated peasants obeyed the ruling classes.

After independence, the upper classes oversaw the nation's political stability and economic growth. After the War of the Pacific (1879–1883)

with Peru and Bolivia, Chile won its mineral-rich northern region. Minerals brought wealth to the country. Leaders used some of the money to develop education, transportation, and other improvements.

Many Chileans realized that, despite economic progress, deep differences existed between the nation's rich and poor. Some advocated an economic system based on capitalism (private ownership). This appealed to those who inherited wealth. Others supported Socialism. They believed that inequalities could be ended only if the state controlled and distributed the fruits of the nation's labor.

The differences among the nation's citizens were obvious at the voting booths after World War II (1939–1945). National elections failed to produce clear-cut winners. In keeping with Chile's constitution, when no candidate won more than half of the total votes, the National Congress certified the person who won the most votes as the winner.

In 1970 the Chilean National Congress appointed Salvador Allende Gossens—who won 36 percent of the popular vote—as the new president.

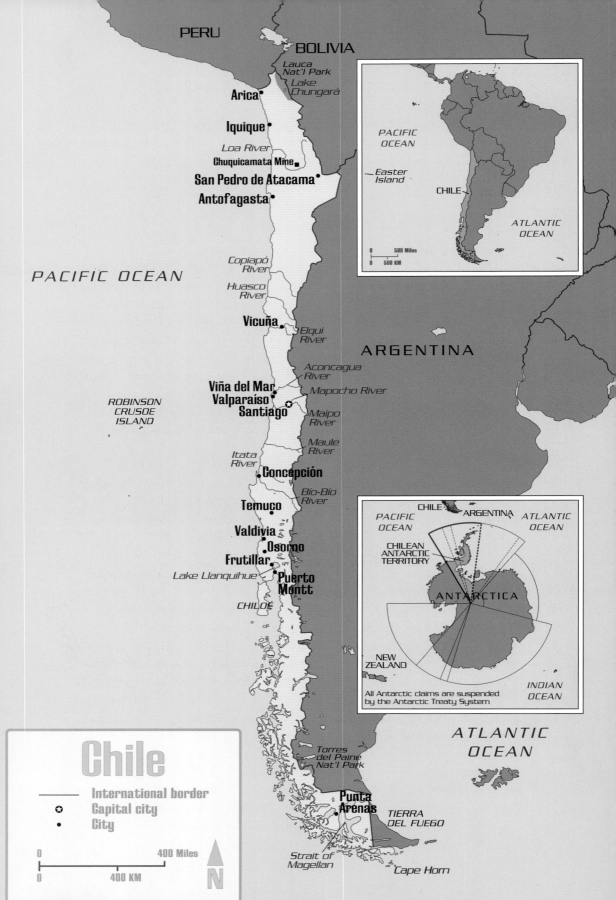

Allende moved quickly to implement Socialism. He placed companies under government control, including copper mining companies that provided the bulk of Chile's wealth. This move caused domestic and international concern. Some people feared that Allende wanted to make Chile a Communist dictatorship. The economy fell into chaos.

In response to the fear and chaos—and with the support of the U.S. Central Intelligence Agency (CIA)—Chile's military leaders violently overthrew the government in 1973. Allende died during the overthrow. Led by General Augusto Pinochet Ugarte, the military arrested, killed, or exiled people they feared.

From 1973 to 1990, Chileans endured military rule. Those in power claimed their harsh repression was the price of protecting the nation from Communism. At first, most Chileans seemed willing to tolerate military rule in order to avoid civil war. This period of rule under Pinochet marked a loss of freedoms, including the right to publicly disagree with leaders. The military regime used fear and threats in its efforts to stamp out political opposition. They executed more than three thousand people during this time. During Pinochet's seventeen-year dictatorship, he also pursued capitalist economic policies. While human rights suffered, the Chilean economy revived. Soon Chile was an economic leader in South America.

Eventually, many people in Chile demanded a more democratic government. In 1988 Chileans voted no to another eight years of Pinochet as president. Under democratically elected presidents, Chile moved successfully from a dictatorship to a democracy. Political stability helped Chile's economy grow rapidly in the 1990s.

The world watched when Pinochet was arrested in Great Britain in 1998. British courts declared the old man too unwell to face trial. He returned to Chile.

Chilean courts have also found Pinochet physically and mentally unfit to stand trial for human rights abuses and financial fraud. Ninety years old in 2006, the general lives under house arrest in Chile. That year Chileans elected their first woman president, Michelle Bachelet Jeria. President Bachelet says the former dictator is no longer politically important. Chile is a country with good natural resources, a strong democracy, and well-educated people. The nation of 16.2 million people is looking to the future.

THE LAND

The Republic of Chile is a land of varied beauty. The long, thin country stretches between the Andes Mountains to the east and the Pacific Ocean to the west. Chile runs 2,650 miles (4,265 kilometers) from north to south. Its average width is about 100 miles (161 km). With 292,135 square miles (756,630 sq. km) of territory, Chile is nearly twice the size of California. The country takes its name from the Indian word *chilli*, which means "where the land ends." True to its name, Chile is the southernmost nation of South America.

Boundaries

The Andes Mountains form Chile's northern and eastern boundaries. The Pacific Ocean runs along Chile's western and southern borders. Chile's neighbors are Peru (north), Bolivia (north and east), and Argentina (east). Antarctica lies about 600 miles (966 km) south of Chile. Chile claims a wedge of the continent—the Chilean Antarctic Territory. Other countries do not accept Chile's claim.

Many islands dot the Pacific coastline toward the southern tip of the country. Chile also owns islands in the Pacific far to the west. These include Easter Island (Rapa Nui), about 2,000 miles (3,219 km) west of Santiago. Also far from the mainland is Robinson Crusoe Island. Chile named it after a novel, *Robinson Crusoe* (1719), by Daniel Defoe. The book is the fictionalized account of a real-life sailor marooned on the island.

◉ The North

A barren region covers Chile from Peru to the Aconcagua River (a distance of about 1,000 miles, or 1,609 km). The Atacama Desert dominates the far north, which Chileans call Norte Grande, or Big North. This desert is one of the driest places on Earth. The land is mostly a flat stretch of sun-baked rocks, broken by arid valleys, salt flats, and treeless mountains. Andean foothills rise near the Bolivian border, leading to high mountain passes. The bleak far north is a treasure-house of

The coarse grasses of the **Atacama Desert** provide food for only the hardiest of animals, such as the vicuña, a type of humpless camel related to the llama.

minerals, especially copper. The Chuquicamata mine in the north is the world's largest open-pit copper mine.

South of the Atacama, the land is less arid. Called Norte Chico, or Little North, it is a transition zone where sparse desert vegetation changes to scrub and occasional forests. The dry soil of the Elqui Valley supports some crops, including grapes.

⊙ The Central Valley

More than 75 percent of Chile's population lives in the Central Valley. Chile's heartland stretches about 600 miles (966 km) from the Aconcagua River south to Puerto Montt. The fertile soil of the region is well suited to farming and cattle raising. Many rivers water the land. One-third of Chile's population lives in the capital city, Santiago. South of Santiago, level farmlands extend to the city of Concepción.

On the southern edge of the Central Valley lies Chile's Lake Country— often called South America's Little Switzerland. The area abounds with snowcapped peaks, sparkling blue lakes, pine-covered slopes, and mountain streams. Temperate rain forests thrive in the wet climate.

⊙ The Southern Zone

The coast of southern Chile is cold and rain swept. Massive walls of granite form fjords (narrow inlets of the sea between cliffs). Ice chunks from glaciers, or slow-moving ice fields, break off and crash thunderously into the sea. Some bluffs along the coast are over 2,000 feet (610 meters) high. Ships find few places to land.

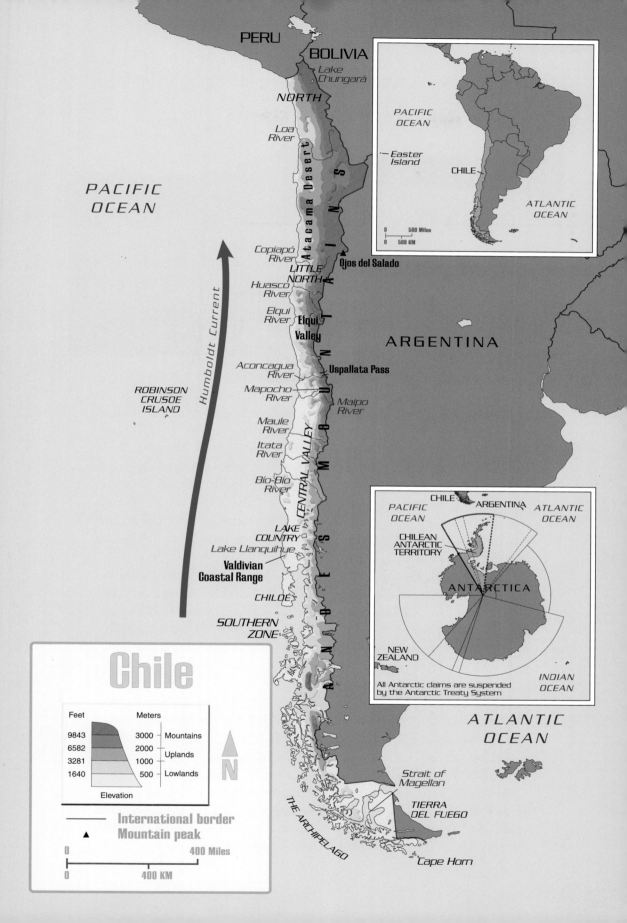

PERU

BOLIVIA

*Lake
Chungará*

PACIFIC
OCEAN

NORTH

*Loa
River*

Atacama Desert

A N D E S   M O U N T A I N S

PACIFIC
OCEAN

Easter
Island

CHILE

ATLANTIC
OCEAN

0   500 Miles
0   500 KM

*Copiapó
River*

▲ Ojos del Salado

*LITTLE
NORTH*

*Huasco
River*

*Elqui
River*

**Elqui
Valley**

*Aconcagua
River*

Uspallata Pass

ARGENTINA

*Mapocho
River*

*Maipo
River*

ROBINSON
CRUSOE
ISLAND

Humboldt Current

*Maule
River*

*Itata
River*

*Bío-Bío
River*

CENTRAL VALLEY

*LAKE
COUNTRY*

Lake Llanquihue

**Valdivian
Coastal Range**

CHILOE

*SOUTHERN
ZONE*

THE ARCHIPELAGO

CHILE   ARGENTINA

PACIFIC
OCEAN

ATLANTIC
OCEAN

CHILEAN
ANTARCTIC
TERRITORY

ANTARCTICA

NEW
ZEALAND

INDIAN
OCEAN

All Antarctic claims are suspended
by the Antarctic Treaty System

ATLANTIC
OCEAN

*Strait of
Magellan*

TIERRA
DEL FUEGO

Cape Horn

Chile

Feet	Meters	
9843	3000	Mountains
6582	2000	Uplands
3281	1000	
1640	500	Lowlands

Elevation

N

——— International border
▲ Mountain peak

0   400 Miles
0   400 KM

The coast of southern Chile has many glaciers and steep-walled fjords.

The Archipelago is an area of hundreds of islands that are the tips of mountains sunk in the ocean. The Archipelago stretches southward for 1,000 miles (1,609 km), from Puerto Montt to Cape Horn.

Southernmost Chile is a twisted maze of inlets, peninsulas, and islands. The town of Punta Arenas lies far south, on the Strait of Magellan—a narrow passageway of water. For most of its history, sheepherders have populated the town. They graze their flocks on the nearby windswept pastures. The discovery of oil near Punta Arenas in 1945 brought oil workers to the area.

Cape Horn lies south of the Tierra del Fuego (Land of Fire) islands, which Chile shares with Argentina. Early European sailors gave the land its name after seeing the native people's fires onshore. The steep, barren rock known as Cape Horn rises 1,391 feet (424 m) out of the sea at the southernmost tip of the continent. Fog usually cloaks the cape, and winds and freezing rains lash it.

Mountains

Mountains cover more than one-third of Chile. In the east, the towering Andes Mountains isolate the country. Snow blocks the mountain passes in the winter. The Andes Mountain chain runs the entire length of South America—about 4,500 miles (7,200 km). It is the world's longest mountain chain. Volcanic eruptions over the past 65 million years formed the Andes. Many Andean volcanoes are still active. In Chile the Andes' snowcapped peaks are highest in the north. The country shares its highest peak—Ojos del Salado—with Argentina. At

22,572 feet (6,880 m), this peak is the second-highest mountain in the Western Hemisphere. Toward the southeast, the Andes decrease in elevation. Even in southernmost Chile, however, peaks rise to more than 6,000 feet (1,829 m).

Mountain ridges also run from the Andes eastward to the coast, creating fertile valleys. The low Valdivian Coastal Range rises along the ocean, parallel to the Andes.

Bodies of Water

The only significant river in the northern desert is the Loa. It empties into the Pacific Ocean north of the Atacama. Lake Chungará, in Lauca National Park, is one of the few lakes in the north. South of the Atacama, several rivers—including the Copiapó, the Huasco, and the Elqui—flow across the region. Some of these rivers are dry for part of the year.

In the Central Valley, many important rivers—including the Maipo, the Maule, the Itata, and the Bío-Bío—go from the Andes to the Pacific. Broad plains flank the rivers, which water farmlands. Santiago is located on the Mapocho River. Snowmelt in the high Andes swells the rivers in the spring. Dams on the swift rivers produce hydroelectric power. Lakes, including Lake Llanquihue, dot the Central Valley's Lake Country.

The Pacific Ocean crashes against Chile's rugged coastline. Chile fronts some of the world's deepest ocean waters. The Peru Current, also called the Humboldt Current, carries cold Antarctic waters up the country's coast. Some parts of Chile's coast, especially in the Central Valley, flatten out into beautiful beaches. But swimming is uncomfortable as the water warms up to only 59°F (15°C) in the summer. At the southern tip of Chile, the Pacific Ocean meets the Atlantic Ocean.

Portuguese explorer Ferdinand Magellan accidentally found the Strait of Magellan in 1520. Winds blew his ships off course, through the strait, and thus around the southern tip of South America. Ship captains have used the twisting, 350-mile (563 km) passageway ever since. The route avoids the even more dangerous and stormy seas around the island of Cape Horn farther south.

Climate

Chile is south of the equator. Seasons there are the reverse of those north of the equator. As a result, Chileans celebrate Christmas in December, in their summer. Because of Chile's varied geography, the country has a complex climate.

The climate in Chile's northern desert is cool because of its high elevation and cold winds from the ocean and the Andes. Temperatures in this region average 69°F (21°C) in January and 57°F (14°C) in July. Rain is rare inland. Near the ocean, sudden summer rains cause flash flooding.

In the Central Valley, the climate in winter (June through August) is chilly and rainy. Summers (December through February) are dry. July temperatures in Santiago average 69°F (21°C), while summer temperatures rarely exceed 84°F (29°C). An average of 14 inches (36 centimeters) of rain falls on Santiago yearly. The rainy Lake Country receives 120 inches (305 cm) of rain yearly.

Southern Chile is cool, windy, and rainy all year. Some places exceed 200 inches (508 cm) of rain annually. This is one of the highest rainfall averages in the world. This region also has one of the stormiest climates in the world. Temperatures in Puerto Montt average 59°F (15°C) in January and 46°F (8°C) in July.

▶ Flora and Fauna

Mountains isolate Chile. Therefore, the country's flora and fauna have evolved differently from the plant and animal life on the rest of the South American continent.

In the north, nothing can survive in the driest areas. Along the northern coast, some plants live on moisture from ocean fog. Spiny trees called *tamarugos* live on little water. Desert brush and grasses and several species of cactus—some found nowhere else in the world—survive in the Andes foothills.

Chile's national flower, the copihue (a lily), thrives in many areas of the country. The potato, which originated in the Andes, grows wild in Chile. Varieties of peppers, beans, and corn are native to Chile.

Chile's temperate (not tropical) rain forests are the world's second largest, after the rain forests of the northwestern United States. South of the Bío-Bío River, forests of beech, laurels, and evergreens

A **giant alerce tree** dwarfs a man in a rain forest near Puerto Montt in southern Chile.

A guanaco roams a northern plateau. Visit www.vgsbooks.com for links to sites to learn more about the different camelids that live in Chile.

cover the land. One of the most distinctive trees in this region is the araucaria, or monkey puzzle tree—a tall evergreen. Alerce trees can live up to four thousand years and are similar to North America's giant redwood trees. Sheep farms are widespread in the southern grasslands.

Wildlife is not as abundant in Chile as it is in other South American countries. Llamas, alpacas, guanacos, and rare vicuñas—all camelids, or humpless relatives of the camel—roam the northern plateaus. Weavers value alpacas for their fleece, once known to the Incas as the fiber of the gods. It was so valuable that only Incan royalty were allowed to wear it. Alpaca fiber is lighter and softer than sheep's wool but five times warmer. It comes in twenty-two natural colors, more than any other animal fiber on Earth.

The chinchilla, a small rodent, is famous for its soft fur. Overhunting has driven the animal nearly to extinction. A similar fate threatens the Andean wolf, the puma, the jaguar, and the guemul—a type of deer native to Chile and featured on the country's coat of arms. The wild, spike-horned pudu—the smallest known deer—stands only 13 inches (33 cm) high. Several kinds of marsupials (mammals with pouches) are native to Chile. The mouse-sized mountain monkey is a marsupial found only in Chile's rain forest.

Chile's Pacific waters teem with more than two hundred species of fish. Many of these fish, such as tuna, are commercially valuable. Marine mammals, including sea lions, otters, and seals, live along the ocean coast.

The country's birds include the condor, albatross, pelican, cormorant, swan, and several kinds of parrots and hummingbirds. Flamingos live in salt flats in the north. The Chilean pigeon and the mockingbird live in the Central Valley. The south is home to the storm petrel, the Humboldt penguin, and the Magellanic penguin.

Natural Resources and Environmental Issues

Chile's northern desert is rich in minerals including iron ore, nitrates, gold, and silver. Copper is Chile's most valuable natural resource. Oil

RING OF FIRE

The Ring of Fire is a zone of Earth that experiences a high number of volcanic eruptions and earthquakes. Most of the ring lies along the 25,000-mile (40,000-km) rim of the Pacific Ocean, including Chile's Pacific coast. Scientists explain the zone's violent earth movements with the theory of tectonic plates. Tectonic plates make up Earth's surface. The rigid plates shift constantly, riding on slow-moving, hot rock. The plates of the Pacific Ocean grind against the surrounding continents' plates. In a process called subduction, the edge of one plate pushes under another. The pressure of subduction causes earthquakes. Volcanoes arise along the edges of subducted plates. Hot gases and molten rock erupt through these openings in Earth's surface.

is found in the extreme south. Chile's forests provide timber. River dams produce electricity. Fishers harvest seafood along the Pacific coastline. Fertile soil in the Central Valley produces ample harvests. Chile's location is also a resource. It sits on the important sea-lanes between the Atlantic and Pacific oceans. Chilean ships guide vessels through the dangerous waters.

Chile benefits economically from its natural resources. But the industries that use the resources threaten the environment. Mining and processing minerals contaminate the soil, air, and water. Fertilizer runoff, raw sewage, industrial waste, and car exhaust add to the pollution. Toxic river water flows into the Pacific Ocean. Deforestation, or the clearing of trees, destroys native forests and their wildlife habitats.

A hole in the ozone layer over Antarctica affects Chile too. The ozone layer absorbs dangerous ultraviolet radiation from the sun. In the spring, the ozone thins, creating a hole in the atmosphere over southern South America. In Punta Arenas, locals check daily postings of ozone levels. They dress to protect themselves from the dangerous ultraviolet light. The ozone hole has grown since the 1960s. Chemicals from human industries and vehicles caused the increase.

Chile's government has been slow to protect the environment but is taking steps to do so. Santiago, for instance, is reducing air pollution by enforcing no-drive days for cars. The city's subway replaces many polluting buses. The government has created national parks and reserves. Protected wilderness areas cover about 18 percent of the country.

Besides human disregard for the environment, Chile also suffers from natural disasters. Earthquakes, volcanic eruptions, and tsunamis, (destructive ocean waves) frequently—and sometimes severely—shake the country. These have taken a heavy toll in damage and in loss of human life throughout Chile's history.

Cities

About 86 percent of Chile's population lives in cities, mostly in the Central Valley. Many Chilean cities are either ports or inland farming or mining centers. Like other countries in Latin America, Chile has undergone rapid urbanization. Most of the people settling in cities come from rural areas. These newcomers often live in crowded one-room shacks that lack running water, sanitation, and electricity. Chileans call these slums *callampas* (mushrooms) because they grow quickly, like mushrooms. Government programs provide for the construction of apartment buildings for low-income Chileans, but adequate housing remains a challenge.

SANTIAGO (population 4.9 million) is the capital of Chile and the nation's largest urban area. Its name means "Saint James" in Spanish. Situated in the Central Valley, Santiago's magnificent setting includes Andean peaks to the east.

Downtown Santiago is a mixture of old, such as the church at left, and new, such as the skyscrapers on the right.

The city features broad, tree-lined avenues, parks, and gardens. Numerous modern office and apartment buildings have been built. Only a few skyscrapers break the horizon because of the danger of earthquakes. Many buildings of historic interest have been restored. Some of them house museums that display reminders of Santiago's long history, beginning with the city's founding in 1541.

Santiago is the seat of the government of Chile. Santiago's privately owned companies produce everything from cloth to computer software. The city's bustling cultural life centers on three universities. College students throng the city's concert halls and theaters. About 25 percent of Santiago's population lives in poverty on the edges of the city.

OTHER CITIES Antofagasta (population 296,000) is Chile's second-largest city. Located on the northern coast, the city receives almost no rain. This port city exports most of the minerals from the northern desert.

Viña del Mar (population 286,000) lies northwest of Santiago. The seaside city, called Viña for short, is Chile's most popular resort. Nearby is Valparaíso (population 279,000). Called the Pearl of the Pacific, it was founded in 1542. It is the country's main port. Because of earthquake destruction, most of the city's buildings are modern.

Temuco (population 245,000) is a fast-growing city in the south. Prosperous farmlands surround Temuco. Nearby are small villages of Mapuche Indians. They are the descendants of the native people who fought Chile's Spanish conquerors. The Mapuche sell their woven garments and crafts at the market in Temuco.

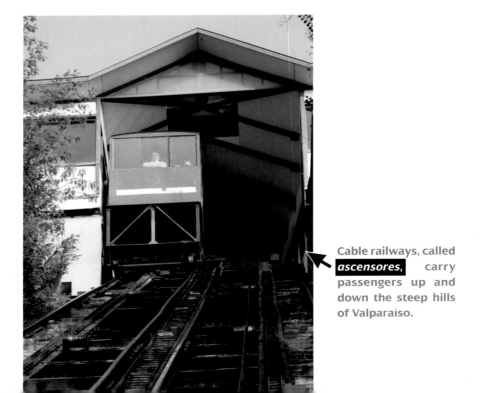

Cable railways, called *ascensores,* carry passengers up and down the steep hills of Valparaíso.

Concepción (population 216,500) is Chile's most important city, after Santiago. The Spanish founded it in 1551. Like the capital, Concepción has a lively cultural scene and university. The city is also one of Chile's main industrial centers and has excellent port facilities. Roads and railways connect Concepción to other Chilean cities.

Two major port cities serve Chile's north. Iquique (population 216,000) is one of the largest port cities in the north. It traces its origins to the nitrate-mining boom of the 1800s. In a famous event in Chile's history, government troops in 1907 killed two thousand workers striking for better wages and conditions in Iquique. After the end of the nitrate boom, citizens of Iquique developed fishing as the city's main industry. Arica (population 185,000) is Chile's northernmost city, near the Peruvian frontier. Like Iquique, it is a thriving center for commercial fishing.

Chile's southernmost large city is Punta Arenas (population 121,000). It sits on the Strait of Magellan at the "end of the world." It is the departure point for ships taking travelers to Antarctica.

LIGHT POLLUTION

Astronomers from around the world come to Chile's northern observatories to study planets, stars, and galaxies. The region's dark, clear night skies are ideal for high-powered, computerized telescopes. Scientists are concerned about the growth of towns in the north, however. The increase in urban population leads to more city lights. Their illumination creates light pollution that blurs images of objects in space. One observatory helped the city of Vicuña install ground-level lighting. By reducing light lost to the sky above, the city not only lowered light pollution but also its electricity bill.

Visit www.vgsbooks.com for links to websites with additional information about the cities in Chile, including population, weather, and what there is to do.

HISTORY AND GOVERNMENT

Scientists believe that the first people in the Americas traveled on a land bridge from Asia to North America about twenty-five thousand years ago. These native peoples eventually migrated to South America. The first settlements in Chile date to about twelve thousand years ago. The largest indigenous (native) group in Chile call themselves Mapuche, which means "people of the land." The Mapuche were farmers and fishers in the Central Valley. They raised corn, squash, beans, and potatoes. The Ona and Yahgan were hunters and fishers in Chile's south. In the north, the Atacama and other small groups were farmers and hunters. They also kept llamas for meat, for fiber, and for carrying burdens. These original Chileans did not keep written records, and historians know little about the eras before the arrival of the Europeans.

In the early A.D. 1400s, the Inca civilization of Peru conquered the northern peoples. The Incas pushed southward into the area near present-day Santiago. However, the Mapuche and smaller groups repeatedly defeated Inca armies and kept them from taking the whole Central Valley.

web enhanced @ www.vgsbooks.com

The Conquest

In 1520 Portuguese explorer Ferdinand Magellan became the first European to see Chile. He sailed past it on his ocean voyage around the world.

In 1532 Francisco Pizarro led a Spanish expedition into Inca territory. He and his men brought with them horses and guns, which the Incas did not have. The Spanish had defeated the Incas by 1533. Lima, Peru, became the seat of Spanish power in the Americas. Spanish viceroys (representatives of the Spanish king) in Lima made Chile part of the Viceroyalty of Peru, a large Spanish colony. Spanish rulers paid little attention to Chile, since—compared to Peru—the colony produced little gold. Also, the native population violently resisted Spanish occupation.

In 1540 the Spaniard Pedro de Valdivia and his men entered Mapuche territory after a difficult march through the Andes. The Mapuche put up a fierce fight. The Spaniards' weapons, however, were more powerful than those of the Mapuche. Therefore, Valdivia and his troops succeeded in establishing Chile's first Spanish settlement at Santiago in 1541.

Defeated in battle but not in spirit, the Mapuche retreated, taking Spanish horses. They continued to mount attacks. Like the Incas, the Spanish failed to overcome Mapuche resistance completely. Within ten years, however, the Spanish established Valparaíso, Concepción, and other cities.

Lautaro was a Mapuche whom the Spaniards captured in their raids to the south. Pedro de Valdivia made the young man his stable groom. But Lautaro escaped, after learning Spanish customs and tactics. On Christmas 1553, he returned with a Mapuche force. They overcame Valdivia and about fifty Spaniards. According to the legend, they killed Valdivia by pouring molten gold down his throat.

Lautaro became the hero of the native people's resistance. The Mapuche resistance continued after his death. However, large numbers of native people throughout Chile died of European diseases such as smallpox.

Spanish Rule

In the early colonial period, the rulers of Spain gave large areas of land in Chile to Spanish colonists. Far away from Europe and isolated by the Andes, Chile attracted only the hardiest settlers. Many were Basques, people from the Pyrenees Mountains in Spain. With little government interference, colonists developed the fertile lands around Santiago. Gradually, they opened up lands farther south. They forced native peoples to work as slaves on the farms. But the land was not suited to the kind of large farms that required huge numbers of workers. Therefore, Chile never brought in large numbers of slaves as other Spanish colonies had done. Many Spanish and indigenous people had children together. People with mixed Spanish and native ancestry came to be called mestizos. The Spanish families looked down on mestizos and indigenous people.

The Spanish colonists brought their Roman Catholic religion and their Spanish language with them. The Catholic Church in Spain also sent missionaries, or religious teachers, to spread Christianity to the native peoples. The church rose in power and influence in Chile. It established schools and owned vast amounts of land. Only Catholic marriages were considered legal.

By 1700 the territory of modern Chile had a population of about 100,000 people. Foremost among these inhabitants were prosperous farmers. They sold their surplus wheat and cattle to the more heavily populated colony of Peru.

Spain forbade Chile and its other colonies to trade with countries other than Spain. Nevertheless, Chileans commonly traded with merchants from several nations. Dutch and British traders, for example, regularly anchored their ships at Chilean ports. They exchanged manufactured goods for Chile's agricultural products.

Independence

In the late 1700s, the successful American and French revolutions inspired Chilean settlers to seek their independence. When Napoleon Bonaparte of France invaded Spain in 1808, Chileans took advantage of Spain's weakness. On September 18, 1810, landowners organized a *cabildo abierto*, or town meeting, in Santiago. Chileans proclaimed their independence from Spain at this meeting. They elected seven people to a national council to oversee the transition of Chile from a colony to an independent nation. However, it would take almost eight more years of struggle before Spain let go of Chile.

Within a year, in July 1811, Chile's first National Congress, or legislative body, assembled. One of its acts was to outlaw slavery. Chile became the second country in the Americas to do so. (Haiti was the first.) At independence, Chile's total population numbered 500,000 people.

Among the lawmakers was the military leader of Chilean patriots, Bernardo O'Higgins Riquelme. Chileans revere him as the Father of Independence. O'Higgins was the son of a Chilean woman and an Irishman, Ambrosio O'Higgins,

Bernardo O'Higgins Riquelme is known as the Father of Chilean Independence.

who served Spain as viceroy of Peru. Ambrosio was not married to Bernardo's mother and had little contact with his son. But he saw to it that Bernardo received a good education in Great Britain.

Bernardo O'Higgins Riquelme

O'Higgins distinguished himself in battle in a joint effort with the Argentine liberator José de San Martín. Together they defeated the Spaniards, who had marched down from the north to reassert control over Chile. In 1817 the Chilean forces beat the Spaniards at the decisive Battle of Chacabuco. The following year, O'Higgins, with San Martín's support, oversaw the drafting of Chile's first constitution. O'Higgins became the country's first president. Chile gained full independence from Spain on February 12, 1818.

Chile's wealthy landowners, the military, and the Catholic Church were the country's main powers. Wealth sharply divided the nation's citizens. The landowners ran large estates. Estate owners provided their farmworkers with small wages, simple housing, and garden plots on the estate. Women and children often worked as servants in the landowners' houses for no pay. Workers mostly had no education and could not vote.

Two main political parties struggled for power in Chile. The Conservative Party wanted to keep Chile as it had been under colonial rule, with the wealthy in charge. The Liberal Party supported rule by representation. Liberals also wanted to limit the power of the Catholic Church and to enact land reform laws to restrict the landowners' power.

From 1817 to 1823, O'Higgins ruled Chile with a firm hand as he pursued his liberal ideals for a more equal society. He tried to break up some huge farm estates and distribute the land to small-scale farmers. O'Higgins further angered wealthy landowners by taxing them heavily. His government used the money to build roads and schools. Several groups resisted his ideas for change in Chile. Liberals charged O'Higgins with not moving quickly enough to create a fair society. Conservatives opposed any change that might disrupt the lifestyle they were used to. The church feared that O'Higgins's efforts to separate church and state would weaken its power. Opposition to his rule became organized, and an open revolt erupted in Concepción. O'Higgins voluntarily left the scene. Disillusioned, he sought exile in Peru, where he later died.

Years of Development

A new constitution in 1833 gave the president far-reaching power and made Catholicism the official religion. Only landowning men older than twenty-five could vote.

Chile's mostly peaceful political evolution was unique among the former Spanish colonies in South America. Early nationhood was a period of bitter fighting in many South American countries. Chile, however, had only four presidents between 1831 and 1871. But a small group of rich, conservative landowners was the real power in the country. Under this group's tight control, the country was unified, and the economy grew.

The first two presidents, José Joaquín Prieto Vial and Manuel Bulnes Prieto, were military men. During their presidencies, with assistance from abroad, Chile established steamship lines and began to mine copper. The country built railroads and introduced the telegraph. Trade with other countries flourished.

Gradually, a new middle class—made up of mining entrepreneurs, bankers, and businesspeople—rose in power. They challenged the traditional domination of the landowners and the Catholic Church. Many of these people were self-made, not inheritors of family power and wealth. They wanted future generations to have the chance to earn success too. With this goal, the middle classes pressured the government into investing heavily in public education. The University of Chile was founded in 1843.

Internal Tensions

Chile's first nonmilitary president, Manuel Montt, held office from 1851 to 1861. During his administration, large numbers of German immigrants arrived in Chile. Mostly farmers, the German newcomers settled the lands of southern Chile. Meanwhile, in the capital city, the decade was far from peaceful. Montt was more controlling than the military presidents before him. He faced civil war twice during his two terms in office.

Manuel Montt

Government forces put down the first revolt soon after Montt's election, but a feud between church and state continued. In seeking to curb the power of the church, Montt angered some of his own supporters, as well as members of the Liberal Party who opposed him. The two groups united to form the Radical Party, which would play a significant role in Chilean politics until the 1970s.

The Montt administration's repression of dissent led to a second revolt and several months of fighting in 1859. Peace was restored only when Montt agreed to the selection of a compromise candidate—José Joaquín Pérez—to succeed him as president.

Pérez ruled from 1861 to 1871. He made liberal reforms. For example, the government improved public services and expanded agriculture. The greatest agricultural growth was in southern Chile, where large numbers of European immigrants had settled.

⬤ The War of the Pacific and Nitrates

By the time Pérez left office, Chile was feeling the impact of a global recession (economic downturn). In 1879 Chile quarreled with neighboring Bolivia over ownership of mineral deposits in the northern desert. The quarrel erupted into the five-year War of the Pacific. Peru also had long-standing disagreements about borders with Chile. Peru joined Bolivia in the war. Chile won a complete victory over both countries in 1883. It also won ownership of the world's largest known deposits of sodium nitrate, a fertilizer. Farmers of other nations demanded huge quantities of this resource. With fertilizer, they would be able to increase their harvests to feed the world's rapidly growing population.

Foreign companies eventually gained control of Chile's nitrate industry. But taxes on nitrate exports increased Chile's earnings enormously. The taxes supplied about half of all government revenues. Chilean leaders used the money to pay for public works. These included the construction of railways, port facilities, and government buildings.

By the late 1800s, Chile's nitrate industry employed nearly fifty thousand workers. Chile's reliance on nitrate (and later, on other mineral exports) changed Chilean politics. The biggest change came from labor unions of miners. The workers organized themselves into unions that strongly influenced national affairs.

Mapuche resistance to outside control had continued for three centuries, costing thousands of lives. Not until 1883 did the Mapuche make their peace with the government of Chile. These native people were moved onto reservations south of the Bío-Bío River.

During the period of nitrate prosperity, presidents found it impossible to impose the old authoritarian style of government. The democratic power of workers and the middle classes forced presidents to bow to the desires of the National Congress. Laws went into effect, for example, that curbed the power of the church. Civil (nonreligious) marriages became legal. Nitrate revenues were invested to improve public education. Prices were high, however, and workers received low pay and worked in poor conditions. The situation led workers to strike for better pay and working conditions. Sometimes strikers met with governmental violence.

Prosperity and industrial growth created jobs in Chile's cities. During this period, rural Chileans flooded cities looking for work. There weren't enough jobs for all of them, however, and many workers did not have the skills to get good jobs. Slums, unemployment, and poverty mushroomed in urban areas, especially in Santiago.

Elected in 1886, President José Manuel Balmaceda pushed for reforms to reduce poverty. Besides challenging the power of the landowners and the Catholic Church, he assigned money for reforms without getting approval from the National Congress. In response, a short but bloody civil war broke out in 1891. More than ten thousand Chilean lives were lost in the fighting before Balmaceda retreated to safety in the Argentine embassy. One month later, his presidential term ended. The day after, Balmaceda wrote a farewell speech and committed suicide.

Thereafter, the growth of many different political parties further weakened the power of the president. Congress increased its power. Chileans enjoyed a free press and continued improvements in public education. But the masses of people remained uneducated and poor.

Economic Decline and Presidential Power

Chile did not take part in World War I (1914–1918). But it made a lot of money selling nitrates. Besides fertilizer, nitrates are used to make explosives. After the war, international markets for Chilean nitrate collapsed because of new, cheaper synthetic fertilizers. Chile's government could no longer use nitrate profits to meet social and economic needs. Dissatisfied, Chileans sought new leadership.

Presidential candidate Arturo Alessandri Palma attracted many voters with his charisma. A gifted public speaker, he expressed the desire that working- and middle-class people had for reform. Alessandri won the 1920 presidential election. Congress, however, blocked his reform programs. When the military sought to control the government, Alessandri resigned in protest in 1924. He left the country for six months, and Chile's armed forces took over the leadership of the divided nation.

A young army officer named Carlos Ibáñez del Campo headed the military junta (ruling group) and oversaw the drafting of a new constitution. It gave more power to the president and less to the National Congress. The government adopted many of Alessandri's reforms, including separation of church and state and freedom of religion. All men older than twenty-one who could read and write became eligible to vote.

By popular demand, Alessandri finished his term when he returned. In 1927 voters elected Ibáñez president. A worldwide economic depression started in 1929. It dragged down the price of copper, and Chile's economy suffered. Ibáñez ruled as a dictator and was overthrown in 1931. Chile then experienced several different governments in fifteen months.

Chileans elected Alessandri president again in 1932. He used his new constitutional powers to restore order. In reaction to Alessandri's crackdown on a labor strike, however, the nation's Communist and Socialist

THE LEFT WING

Communism is a political system that aims to create economic fairness. It promotes common ownership of all goods, instead of private ownership. Socialism is less extreme. Socialists believe that the state should control the way goods and services are produced and distributed. They believe in some private ownership of property. Both Communists and Socialists are called left-wing, or leftist, groups. They consider equality and the common good to be more important than individual freedom. "Right wing" refers to conservatives, who emphasize freedom more than equality. Moderates are called middle of the road, or centrists. The terms come from the French Revolution (1789–1799). The most radical lawmakers sat on the left-hand side of the French legislature, while the most conservative sat on the right.

parties organized the leftist Popular Front Party. This coalition (multiparty group) unified the Radical Party and Socialist and Communist parties. Women won the right to vote in 1935. With strong backing from labor unions, the Popular Front ran a candidate for the presidency in 1938. Out of a total of 450,000 votes cast, the coalition candidate, Pedro Aguirre Cerda, won by 4,000 votes.

Chileans remember President Aguirre for his innovative social policies. He said he wanted to set forth programs to provide food, shelter, and other necessities to Chileans. But a massive earthquake in 1939 slowed government improvements. Resources went instead to help the victims of the earthquake. The quake killed more than 60,000 people and left 750,000 others without homes. Nevertheless, Aguirre made reforms, including labor laws and welfare measures that benefited Chilean workers and their families. A young doctor named Salvador Allende Gossens served as Aguirre's minister of health. Aguirre also opened Chile's doors to Spaniards fleeing Spain after the end of the Spanish Civil War (1936–1939). He employed famous poet Pablo Neruda to supervise the refugee program. By the time Aguirre died in office of natural causes in 1941, he had become one of the most popular presidents in Chilean history.

Chile was neutral at first in World War II. President Juan Antonio Ríos made Chile an important supplier of copper, nitrates, and other war goods for the fight against Nazi Germany. In 1942 Chile joined the Allies fighting against Germany and Japan.

◉ Political Disunity

When Ríos died in office, Gabriel Gonzáles Videla—a leader of Aguirre's Radical Party—won the national elections in 1946. At first, he headed a coalition government composed of Communist, Socialist, and Liberal Party members. In 1948, however, he purged the government of Communists—including Pablo Neruda, who went into exile.

Pablo Neruda

The 1952 election failed to produce a majority winner, demonstrating Chileans' political divisions. Congress certified Carlos Ibáñez del Campo, the military officer who had ruled Chile dictatorially from 1927 to 1931, as the nation's new president. Ibáñez, who was in his mid-seventies, proved unable to cope with high inflation and the rising tide of popular discontent. Chileans blamed foreign interests who owned copper mines—especially U.S corporations—for the nation's ills.

Jorge Alessandri Rodríguez, the son of former president Arturo Alessandri, succeeded Ibáñez. From 1958 to 1964, Alessandri stabilized economic problems. He also initiated housing and agricultural reform programs in response to popular demands. But the gap between the nation's poor and rich did not get smaller. Adding to the country's problems, in 1960 Chile's worst earthquake caused massive damage and loss of life.

Promises to expand reform programs and to get more profits for Chile from foreign-owned copper companies helped Eduardo Frei Montalva win the presidency in 1964. Frei was the first Latin American president elected as a candidate of the Christian Democratic Party. He was also the winner by the largest margin in Chile since 1931. He got 56 percent of the popular vote. As president from 1964 to 1970, Frei undertook a program of social and economic reform that he called a Revolution in Liberty. However, he was not able to curb Chile's growing inflation.

Salvador Allende Gossens

◉ Salvador Allende Gossens

By the time President Frei left office, his own party had become divided over how it should achieve reforms. These differences contributed to the presidential victory in 1970 of Salvador Allende Gossens. He promised to bring Socialism to Chile and to maintain democracy. Allende became the first democratically elected Marxist to serve as head of state in the Western Hemisphere.

(Marxists are followers of the political ideas of Karl Marx, the founder of Communism.)

Allende did not enjoy majority support in the National Congress. But he immediately set out to transform Chile into a Socialist state. He nationalized (converted from private to state ownership) approximately eighty major firms, including all of Chile's largest banks and industries. Most importantly, Allende nationalized the copper industry, which U.S. companies had dominated. He offered almost no payment to the foreign companies in exchange. In response, the United States imposed an economic blockade on Chile. This shutdown of trade had a huge impact. Chile's economic difficulties worsened.

Some people feared that Allende was determined not only to make Chile a Socialist state but a Communist one. Allende's efforts to impose socialism did not use violence or impose censorship. But the president's friendship with Cuban Communist dictator Fidel Castro fed fears of Communism. The anti-Communist U.S. CIA secretly supported activities against Allende with money and advice.

Allende's attempts to create an equal society were an economic disaster. Inflation soared in Chile. Widespread shortages of food and goods

Chilean army troops fire on the Presidential Palace in Santiago on September 11, 1973. The coup, led by General Pinochet, overthrew the Socialist government of President Salvador Allende. Allende died inside the palace.

sparked strikes and violence. A two-month truckers' strike closed down Chile's supply lifelines. The country was in crisis. With Chileans divided, Chile's armed forces staged a coup (violent overthrow of the government) on September 11, 1973. The military bombed the Presidential Palace. The CIA-supported coup resulted in Allende's death. Apparently, he committed suicide rather than be captured. The Chilean military immediately arrested, exiled, or executed thousands of Allende's supporters.

Pinochet and Military Rule

Chileans were shocked by the bloodshed in their democratic nation. Many, however, welcomed military rule. They hoped that strict leadership would end the disorder of Allende's time. General Augusto Pinochet Ugarte headed Chile's new military junta. He also led the army.

Once in power, the junta dissolved the National Congress and banned all political activity. Four members of the junta exercised legislative power. But Pinochet was the real ruler. The junta appointed all local leaders, including governors, mayors, and university presidents. The military also imposed a state of siege. This gave the government power to arrest, detain, and jail protesters without trial.

The junta members silenced people who disagreed with them. They subjected political opponents to threats, jailings, and torture. Some prisoners were later released or were permitted to leave the country. Others simply disappeared. (Later it became known the military killed them and dumped many in the sea.) Pinochet declared that his actions

Many of Pinochet's economic advisers studied at the University of Chicago with Nobel Prize-winning economist Milton Friedman. Economists study how goods and services are made and distributed. Friedman taught free-market economics. In this system, the government plays the smallest role possible in the economy. Chileans called Pinochet's advisers the Chicago Boys.

and orders were necessary to save the country from Communism.

The Catholic clergy were the only organized group who managed to keep speaking out against Pinochet's regime. Against government orders, the church ran a prisoner relief agency that tried to locate people who had disappeared. It counted 750 disappearances in 1975 alone. The regime arrested priests and nuns they suspected of dissent.

Under Pinochet, Chile's human rights suffered. But the economy improved. Pinochet employed a group of economists. With their advice, Chile's economy experienced a high growth rate during much of the 1970s. Many Chileans supported Pinochet because of the country's financial boom. Pinochet paid foreign companies for their lost copper holdings, but he kept Chilean control of copper mines. This was a popular decision.

The military returned to the original owners much of the land that the Allende government had given to poor farmers. Eventually, the landowning families from colonial times again owned most of Chile's richest farmland. Running the farms as big businesses with modern farm technology, the landowners greatly increased farm export profits. Farmers who lost their small plots continued to move to the cities, where work was hard to find.

As the economy improved, society stabilized, and the government relaxed its rule. The junta lifted the state of siege in 1978, and it allowed the return of some Chileans who had fled the country in 1973. Tolerance of public criticism of the government increased, and arrests decreased.

Voters in 1980 approved a new constitution that gave General Pinochet another eight years as president. Many Chileans did not vote in the election, protesting the lack of democratic options. However, constitutional changes also made plans for a democratic government in the future.

During the early 1980s, the worldwide economy took a turn for the worse. Chile's economy also went downhill. The nation's unemployment rate reached historic highs. Cutbacks in welfare programs were felt throughout the nation. Lack of government rules had allowed banks to borrow and lend more money than borrowers could pay back. The banking system was in danger of failing.

Unhappy with their government and the economy, Chileans began to demand a return to democracy. Catholic clergy spearheaded a democracy movement called the National Assembly of Civil Society. It gathered a diverse group of Chileans, including teachers, students, businesspeople, and labor union members.

The move for democracy suffered a setback in 1986, after a failed assassination attempt on Pinochet. Afterward, the junta imposed a state of siege for reasons of national security. The government proceeded to tap telephones, to censor the press, and to hold prisoners at secret locations. The junta also banned public gatherings.

By 1988 the economy had improved again. That year another vote was held to determine if Pinochet would continue in power for eight more years. Chileans were asked to vote simply yes or no. The general was confident of his success. The Chilean people, however, voted no.

Visit www.vgsbooks.com for links to websites with additional information about Chile's history, government, political leaders, and current events.

Return to Democracy

Pinochet announced that elections would occur in 1989. Voters chose Patricio Aylwin Azócar to serve a four-year transitional term as president.

Patricio Aylwin Azócar speaks at a campaign rally before winning the 1989 Chilean presidential election.

On election night, Chileans took to the streets celebrating the end of seventeen years of military rule. Pinochet reluctantly gave up his rule, but he refused to resign as army commander in chief.

Aylwin is a member of the Coalition for Parties for Democracy, called the Concertación Coalition. It is a group of Socialist and centrist political parties. He kept many of the economic policies from Pinochet's time. But he gave far greater attention to social issues. To aid the poor, for example, Aylwin's government raised workers' minimum wage. People starting small businesses received help. By improving education and job training, the government increased employment. Many poor Chileans began to make a better living.

The president also appointed a special commission to investigate crimes that the armed forces committed during Pinochet's regime. The commission reported that military officials had murdered more than three thousand Chileans. After the investigation, outraged citizens demanded that Pinochet and his men be prosecuted for these crimes. Pinochet—with his power as head of the army—granted amnesty (official pardon) to the military for human rights abuses that took place during military rule. Therefore, guilty officers went unpunished.

In 1994 Eduardo Frei Ruíz Tagle, the son of a former Chilean president, became Chile's next civilian president. He reduced the military's role in government and supervised Chile's healthy economy.

In 1998 Pinochet resigned as army commander in chief. He became a senator for life, something the constitution allowed former presidents to do. As a senator, he was immune, or legally protected, from prosecution for any crimes. In October of that year, he flew to Great Britain for medical treatment. There, the British government

A **protester** in Great Britain celebrates Pinochet's arrest.

arrested him, after Spain requested his extradition (the handover of a criminal for trial). Pinochet entered into a long legal battle in the British courts.

The Twenty-First Century

In March 2000, President Ricardo Lagos took office. He was Chile's first Socialist president since Allende. That same month, Great Britain said Pinochet's health was too poor for him to stand trial. He was allowed to return to Chile. The next year, a Chilean court ruled that Pinochet should stand trial for covering up human rights abuses. He was placed under house arrest. But in July 2002, Chile's Supreme Court declared Pinochet mentally unfit for trial. All charges against him were dropped. Four days later, he stepped down as senator, blaming poor health.

When Spain requested the extradition of Pinochet from Great Britain, it was acting on the United Nations' International Convention against Torture. This agreement says that torture is a crime against humanity. Therefore, one country can request the arrest in a second country of someone accused of torture in a third country.

Chile's environmental issues came to public attention during Lagos's presidency. Industrial and urban growth in recent years had caused a rise in pollution and a rapid loss of forests. Concerned people staged protests, some of them violent, against mining, logging, and a proposed dam on the Bío-Bío River. The dam threatens Mapuche land. Furthermore, the Mapuche demanded the return of land that had belonged to their ancestors. Lagos set up a commission to investigate the Mapuche demands. The commission recommended that the constitution give more rights to Chile's native population. However, in 2003, the National Congress rejected any such changes to the constitution. Mapuche and environmental activists continued their protests, but work on the dam went forward.

In 2004 Chileans saw justice done when Manuel Contreras, the former head of Pinochet's secret police, was tried. The court found him guilty of the 1974 death of a journalist. The Supreme Court stripped Pinochet of his immunity, but once again, courts declared him too unwell for trial. Congress also voted to end the right of former presidents to become senators for life. That year President Lagos defied the powerful Catholic Church by signing a law giving Chileans the right to divorce. The church opposes divorce. It also opposes abortion, which remains illegal in Chile.

In January 2006, Chile's conservative society saw more changes. Voters elected the country's first woman president. Michelle Bachelet

Chileans hold signs and banners at a rally for **Michelle Bachelet Jeria** in 2006.

Jeria became the fourth president in a row from the center-left Concertacion coalition. She had served as minister of defense and health under President Lagos. After she was sworn in, in March 2006, Bachelet chose equal numbers of women and men to be members of her cabinet (group of government advisers). Besides working for a more equal society, Bachelet says she will continue Chile's free-market economic policies. These policies have made Chile's economy one of the healthiest in Latin America. Despite improvements, 20 percent of Chileans still live in poverty.

President Michelle Bachelet's father was an air force general who opposed the 1973 military coup. He died in prison, after being tortured. Bachelet and her mother were also in prison briefly and tortured. Afterward, the Pinochet regime forced them to leave Chile. They returned in 1979.

◉ Government

Chile's constitution was passed in 1980 and has been amended several times, including in 2005. All Chilean citizens eighteen years and older are eligible and required to vote.

A president elected by the people heads Chile's executive branch. The president is both the chief of state and the head of government. Presidents serve one six-year term. The president appoints a cabinet of twenty ministers to run the day-to-day operation of the government.

The Chilean legislature, called the National Congress, consists of two houses. One hundred twenty members serve in the Chamber of Deputies. They are elected to four-year terms. The thirty-eight elected members of the Senate serve eight-year terms. After an election, the outgoing government names nine of the total forty-seven senators.

The twenty-one-member Supreme Court heads Chile's judicial branch. The president appoints the court's judges from lists drawn up by the court. The Senate must ratify the president's choice. The Constitutional Court rules on laws and amendments to the constitution. Chile's legal system is based on Spanish law. In 2005 Chile installed a new criminal justice system. It is modeled after the U.S. system.

For administrative purposes, Chile is divided into twelve regions, plus the region of Santiago. These regions, in turn, are subdivided into fifty-one provinces and three hundred counties.

THE PEOPLE

Chile is home to 16.2 million people. The nation's population is steadier in numbers than most Latin American countries. A national commission to promote family planning has existed since 1974. Chilean women have an average of two children each. Since 24 percent of Chile's population is younger than fifteen, the number of young women entering their childbearing years continues to grow. As a result, the population will continue to grow too. Chile's projected population for 2025 is 19 million. The government is satisfied with the country's growth rate.

The United Nations' Human Development Index (HDI) ranks Chile 43 out of the 177 ranked countries. The HDI measures human well-being, or the prospects of a person having a long, healthy life with education and a good standard of living. The UN states that it is not a measure of happiness. Key indicators such as life expectancy, literacy, and average income determine the HDI. The United States ranks 8 out of 177. Spain ranks 20. Chile's neighbors rank 34 (Argentina), 85 (Peru), and 114 (Bolivia).

● Population Distribution

Chile's population density is 55 people per square mile (21 per sq. km). This is about average for South America. The population density in North America is 43 people per square mile (17 per sq. km).

Chile's population is unevenly distributed. About 86 percent of all Chileans live in urban areas. More than 75 percent of the people inhabit the Central Valley. Clusters of people live in and around the region's ports and mining settlements as well as in the cities that serve surrounding agricultural areas. More than 33 percent of the total population resides in the capital city of Santiago and its surrounding communities. Few people live in the dry north, the harsh Andes, or the islands and forests of the cold, stormy south.

● Ethnic Groups

Chile's people are mostly ethnically unified. Most people are descended from different groups who intermixed during the colonial era.

Most of the people in Chile are **mestizos.** These Chileans are mingling in the main square, the Plaza de Armas, in Santiago.

Mestizos make up 75 percent of the population. Most of these people of mixed European and native ancestry have Spanish backgrounds. But some have British, Irish, German, or African ancestors.

About 20 percent of Chile's population are unmixed immigrants and their descendants. They are primarily from Spanish backgrounds, but descendants of German settlers are a small percentage too. Many of Chile's German immigrants settled in the southern provinces, particularly around the cities of Puerto Montt, Osorno, and Valdivia. Italian, French, and Middle Eastern immigrants, mostly Palestinian, also figure as ethnic minorities.

Members of Chile's indigenous groups comprise about 5 percent of the population. The Mapuche make up 87 percent of the native population. Their ancestors led the resistance against the Spanish for three hundred years. Most live in cities, but about 20 percent of them live isolated from the rest of the population on reservations south of the Bío-Bío River. A small number of Aymara live in northern Chile, near the border of Peru and Bolivia. Their name means "children of the sun." They cross freely between Chile and Bolivia, in a region that has been theirs

The Spanish called all native peoples in Chile *Araucanians.* The name Araucanian is from *arauca*, the Inca word for "enemy." In reality, there are many different native groups. The Mapuche make up the largest group.

for generations. Atacameños and Quechua are other small indigenous groups. Quechua live in the most isolated mountains near Peru and in Peru. On Easter Island, two-thirds of the 3,800 inhabitants are Rapa Nui. They are descendants of the original Polynesian inhabitants. A few native people in Chile speak the language of their ancestors, but most speak Spanish.

Education

Chile has a history of a strong commitment to education, beginning with schools the Catholic Church started in colonial times. Chile's national government founded the University of Chile in 1842 in Santiago. The university quickly became one of the most respected in Latin America.

The modern government of Chile spends a large amount—about 16 percent—of its budget on education. As a result, more than 96 percent of Chileans can read and write. This is one of the highest literacy rates in South America. That figure climbs to 99 percent among Chileans aged 15 to 24. About the same percentage of men and women are literate. Elementary school attendance is free and compulsory from the ages of 6 to 15. A number of special schools serve the handicapped, and classrooms for the very poor are often located in low-income neighborhoods. The country's teachers are well trained. Primary

THE MEANING OF TINGO

Most world languages have some words with no English equivalents. Author Adam Jacot de Boinod collected some of these words in his book *The Meaning of Tingo* (Penguin Press, 2006). *Tingo* is a word from Pascuense, a language spoken on Chile's Easter Island. It means "to borrow objects, one at a time, from a friend's house until there is nothing left." In the same language, *hakamaru* means "not to return borrowed items until the owner asks for them back."

Two schoolgirls walk to school in Valparaíso. Children wear school uniforms in Chile. In fact, Chilean high schoolers are referred to as penguins because of their black-and-white uniforms.

school classes usually are quite small, with only about twenty pupils. Classes are taught in Spanish, the official language of Chile

Private high schools charge fees, and public high schools are free. Far fewer students attend high school than elementary school. Most high-school-age children have to get jobs to help provide for their families. Therefore, high school students mainly come from well-off families.

Vocational training, which can take anywhere from three to seven years to complete, is provided at industrial and commercial secondary schools in urban areas. Agricultural schools in rural areas offer seven-year programs.

The higher-education system includes more than thirty colleges. The University of Chile and the State Technical University—both with branches throughout the nation—account for about half of the total university enrollment. Some Chileans study abroad, mostly in the United States or Europe. The most popular professions among young Chileans are teaching, medicine, mining, and engineering.

Founded in 1843, The **University of Chile,** was one of the first universities in the world to admit women. A statue of Andrés Bello, the first rector, or director, of the university sits in front of the school.

Health

Average life expectancy at birth is 76 years among Chileans. Females can expect to live 79 years and males about 73 years. These figures are a little higher than the average life expectancy in South America and a little lower than the life expectancy in North America. In Chile, as in other industrialized nations around the world, the major killers are cancer and heart disease. Alcoholism and cocaine use are of growing public concern. The infant mortality rate (IMR, the number of babies who die after birth) is 8 per 1,000. This is the lowest IMR in South America. The IMR in North America is 7 deaths per 1,000 babies.

Chile's HIV rate is 0.3 percent. HIV causes the deadly disease AIDS. It is transmitted through body fluids, usually through sex or intravenous drug use. Modern drugs increase the survival rates for people with HIV, but the drugs are very expensive.

ALTITUDE SICKNESS

At high altitudes (elevations more than 5,000 feet [1,524 m] above sea level), the oxygen content of air decreases. In the mountains, less oxygen reaches the brain and muscles, forcing the heart and lungs to work harder. Chileans who live in high places are used to the thin air. But Acute Mountain Sickness (AMS) frequently strikes tourists in the Andes. AMS causes headaches and dizziness. It can also cause more severe symptoms such as coughing blood and irrational behavior. In extreme cases, it can even lead to death.

Except for the urban and rural poor, most Chileans enjoy good health care. Chile has 846 hospitals and more than nineteen thousand doctors. The government emphasizes programs in infant care. Government-sponsored school lunches feed economically deprived children. A surplus of physicians, dentists, and health personnel exists in the Santiago area. Authorities encourage some of these professionals to move to other areas of the country, where medical services are in short supply.

Ways of Life

Chile has a fairly conservative and formal society. People usually dress and behave modestly. Clothing styles are similar to those in North America and Europe. Chileans value serious and somber behavior in public. In general, they do not display the expressive behavior common in much of Latin America.

Traditional values are strong in Chile, and the family is the central and most important unit in society. Chileans usually marry in their mid-twenties and have children soon after marriage. Many women work outside the home, but they still put family first. Women have a degree of power in society because of their family roles. They also are gaining power in public roles.

Most Chileans live in cities. People who live in the country mostly farm small plots of land or are laborers on large estates. Some work as herders on sheep farms. Rural people often live in poverty with limited social services. Therefore, many continue to migrate to cities looking for work.

Chilean women greet other women and men with a slight kiss on the right cheek. Men greet one another with handshakes.

A wide gap exists between the lives of the very poor and the very rich in Chile. Migrants from the countryside often live in poor neighborhoods on the edges of Santiago and other big cities. Slum dwellers construct housing out of found materials and live without running water, electricity, or paved roads. Government programs in recent years have replaced some slums with modern housing. Clean water and other public services improve the standard of living. But government housing is far from the center of the cities, and workers must travel a long way to their jobs. Many working-class people find

Many Chileans still live in **slums,** such as this one outside of Valparaíso.

employment in mines and factories. They also may work as maids, gardeners, sales clerks, or in other low-paying jobs.

Middle-class people in Chile's cities find housing in apartment buildings or modest single-family houses. They may work as teachers, nurses, office workers, or government workers. The upper classes live in modern luxury apartment buildings of glass and steel or in large houses, sometimes of colonial Spanish style with red-tile roofs. Their homes may have large gated gardens and lawns, tended by gardeners. Often the wealthy have beach houses near the ocean. Traditionally, the richest Chileans were mine owners or owners of large rural estates who ran their businesses from the city. These families still exist, but new wealth has come from jobs in finance and business.

Middle-class Chileans have modest homes or apartments. These are on a hillside in Valparaíso.

Visit www.vgsbooks.com for links to websites with additional information about the people of Chile, including the different ethnic and social groups that live there.

CULTURAL LIFE

Spanish and other European traditions have been the main influences on Chile's culture. Little remains of pre-Conquest indigenous cultures. In the 1960s, Chile developed a cultural movement that revived folk and native music. Its influence remains alive in Chile. Folk art also flourishes. The nation is most famous for its poets and other writers.

The military government of 1973 to 1990 enforced censorship and silenced many voices in the nation. Many artists, musicians, and writers became popular overseas as champions of social justice. The grim realities of life under dictatorship are reflected in Chilean expressions during this time and afterward. In the twenty-first century, many cultural forms thrive in Chile.

Religion and Holidays

The government separated the powers of church and state in 1925, and religious freedom is guaranteed. Almost 80 percent of Chileans are members of the Roman Catholic faith. Most Catholics in Chile say

they do not attend church regularly. However, the Catholic Church has been a dominant player in Chile's history and society. For instance, divorce was not legal in Chile until 2004, largely because of the church's influence.

About 12 percent of the Chilean people belong to Protestant churches. German immigrants brought Lutheranism to Chile. Baptists and Methodists are other Protestant denominations in the country. Evangelical Christianity is a rapidly growing religious force in Chile. It gains membership through missionary activities in communities and on television. About half a million Latter-day Saints (also called Mormons) exist in Chile. About 6 percent of Chileans claim no religious affiliation.

Less than 2 percent of Chileans practice other religions. A small number of Jews live mostly in the Santiago area. Middle Eastern immigrants often belong to the Islamic faith. And some native peoples practice the traditional religion of their ancestors. Their beliefs are based on the spiritual powers of nature. These powers are either good or bad, creating harmony or chaos. Spiritual leaders are believed to be able to communicate with the spiritual world. For instance, if someone is ill, the spiritual leader seeks to restore harmony and bring about healing. A sacred drum, called the *kultrun*, is part of Mapuche ceremonies.

Holidays in Chile are like those of other countries in the Western Hemisphere. Family and community festivals mark Christmas, Independence Days (September 18–19), Columbus Day (October 12), and New Year's Day. Because Christmas and New Year's Day fall in the summer, Chileans often celebrate outdoors. Chileans are less given to the extravagant celebration of religious holidays than are the peoples of other Latin American countries. For example, Holy Week (the week before Easter) is the occasion for just two holidays in Chile. In contrast, many other South American countries observe the entire week.

The Arts

Many Chilean painters and sculptors have received international attention. Roberto Matta (1911–2002) is Chile's best-known painter. He moved to Europe as a young man and worked with famous surrealist painters such as Salvador Dali. Matta's art expresses a respect for human value in the face of war and machines.

Violeta Parra (1917–1967) is best known as a folk singer, but she was also a visual artist. Folk styles inspired her art as they did her music. She painted and wove *arpilleras*—decorative tapestries common in Chile and other Latin American countries. Her animals, people, and plants took on fanciful, magical forms.

Chileans produce beautiful silver objects. Jewelers make items from silver and lapis lazuli (a blue stone that is found only in Chile and Afghanistan). The Mapuche are skilled silversmiths. Their ancestors were working in silver long before Europeans arrived.

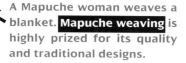

A Mapuche woman weaves a blanket. **Mapuche weaving** is highly prized for its quality and traditional designs.

Indigenous Andean peoples make beautiful knitted items with traditional designs.

▶ Literature

Since the late 1500s, literature has been Chile's most famous cultural expression. The greatest Spanish epic of that time was *La Araucana*, written in Chile by Alonso de Ercilla y Zúñiga (1534–1594). He was a Spanish soldier and poet who kept a diary of the warfare with the Mapuche.

The 1800s saw the development of realism, a literary style that portrays the way people really act. Chilean realists included novelists Alberto Blest Gana and Baldomero Lillo. An enduring realist classic is Eduardo Barrios' novel *The Child Who Went Crazy with Love* (1915). Barrios was interested in the inner life of unusual or abnormal characters.

Two Chilean poets have won the Nobel Prize for Literature. In 1945 Gabriela Mistral (1889–1957) became the first Latin American to win this prize. She was an educator who studied folklore and children's songs and chants. Her most famous collections of poetry include *Desolation* (1922) and *Tenderness* (1924).

Pablo Neruda (1904–1973) won the Nobel Prize in 1971. Neruda's poetry is well known around the world. His most popular collection is *Twenty Love Songs and a Song of Despair*, published when he was twenty. Neruda's poetry gained more readers after the release of the popular Italian film *Il Postino* (The Postman, 1995). The film was based on the novel *Burning Patience* by Chilean Antonio Skarmeta (b. 1940). The story imagines a friendship between Neruda and a simple postman who wants to use poetry to win a woman's love.

Few Chileans of the past or present approach the popularity of Mistral and Neruda. Even Chileans who are not particularly well read honor these two cultural heroes and quote from their verses.

MONSTER BABIES

Native peoples in Chile have a rich storytelling tradition. In Chiloé (a group of isolated southern islands), frightening tales of wizards and magic abound. Especially gruesome are stories about the *inbunches* who guard the wizards' caves. These monsters were once human babies. Witches stole them and broke all their bones, sewed all their bodily openings shut, and changed them into creatures that feed on blood.

Visit www.vgsbooks.com for links to websites with additional information about Chile's literary history and the works of Chile's writers. Chile, nicknamed the Land of Poets, is home to many great authors.

Chile and much of Latin America saw the rise of a literary phenomenon called the Boom in the 1970s. Novelists of this period enjoyed a huge increase in readership worldwide. Many writers of the Boom era developed a style called magic realism. This style weaves dreams and fantastic elements into the fabric of everyday reality. José Donoso (1924–1996) was a Boom novelist in Chile. His novel *Coronation*, like his other works, deals with individuals in a changing society. The main character is the last of a crumbling, wealthy family. He falls in love disastrously with a young native girl. Chilean Silvio Caiozzi directed the 2000 film version of this novel.

Ariel Dorfman is a Chilean writer who recorded the events around the Allende era. In his play *Death and the Maiden,* a woman meets a man she believes tortured her during the military dictatorship years ago. In 1994 the play was made into an English-language film, starring Sigourney Weaver and Ben Kingsley.

Isabel Allende (b. 1942) is the most famous of Chile's many living writers. Her work is available in many languages. She is a relative of former president Salvador Allende. Her first novel, *The House of the Spirits* (1982), was a best seller and brought her international fame. The story follows the loves, spirituality, and politics of the colorful Trueba family. Allende uses magical realism to create a world of both spirits and living people. Hollywood adapted *The House of the Spirits* into a film (1993) starring Winona Ryder and Antonio Banderas. *My Invented Country* (2003) is Allende's nonfiction memoir of her family and her country. She also wrote a trilogy for young readers. *Forest of the Pygmies* (2005) is the last of the three volumes. The stories follow the adventures of friends Alexander and Nadia. Their magical abilities include turning into a jaguar and an eagle.

The younger generation of novelists includes Alberto Fuguet, Andrea Maturana, Pedro Lemebel, and Ana Maria del Rio. Many deal with social realities, such as drugs and sexuality. Del Rio's novel for young adults, *Carmen's Rust*, presents the grim life story of a teenage girl.

◉ Film

Chilean film production has grown since the mid-1990s. Chilean filmmakers produce films that are popular at home and receive acclaim abroad. *Soccer Stories* (1997),

TELENOVELAS

As in other Latin American countries, *telenovelas*, or soap operas, are very popular in Chile. Telenovela stories last for several months and air at night. When one series ends, the actors reappear as different characters in the next one. All levels of society and both sexes watch and discuss them. Modern plots explore social topics such as AIDS and unwed mothers.

directed by Andres Wood, was a box-office hit in Chile. It relates three tales revolving around the nation's favorite sport. The tales are funny but also offer a critique of Chile's social problems, such as poverty. In the second tale, a poor boy finds a soccer ball. When he loses his mother's money in a soccer game, he is forced to sell the ball. *Dark Angel* (2000) by writer-director Jorge Olguín met great success in Chile as the country's first horror film. *Taxi for Three* (2001) by writer-director Orland Lubbert exposes Santiago's slums. The film relates the sometimes lighthearted story about two crooks who involve a taxi driver in their robbery spree. *Play* represented Chile in the 2005 Academy Awards. It is the first feature film by writer-director Alicia Scherson. Her story follows two people searching for love one summer day in Santiago.

Alicia Scherson

Music

Chile has a long history of folk music and of music expressing social and political concerns. The legendary Violeta Parra was an important Chilean composer and performer. Her popularity in Chile is similar to Elvis Presley's in the United States. In the 1960s, she led a revival of Chilean folk music. The revival is called Nueva Canción, meaning "New Song." It expressed great hopes for justice in Chile. Its blend of modern lyrics with traditional tunes and instruments spread throughout South America, and its influence continues. Parra's song "Gracias a la Vida" (Thanks to Life) became one of the best-known songs from Latin America. Singer Joan Baez's performance of the song made it popular in the United States. Parra's children Isabel and Angel Parra performed with Baez. They continue their mother's musical legacy.

Nueva Canción became associated with political activism on behalf of the villagers and the native people from which the music sprang. Many performers supported Salvador Allende and his reforms. "You Can't Have a Revolution Without Songs" was a popular motto for musicians in this era. Victor Jara (1932–1973), a New Song musician and poet, was one of the premier performers who supported the Allende presidency. During the 1973 coup, soldiers beat him to death.

After the military takeover in 1973, Pinochet banned public performances and radio play of songs that criticized the junta. Musicians played in secret. Touring groups of Chilean musicians gained popularity abroad.

Illapu and Inti-Illimani are two Andean folk music groups who perform widely. Both groups are active in the twenty-first century.

These **folksingers and dancers** perform in traditional Spanish clothing.

Illapu means "lightning bolt" in Quechua. *Inti-Illimani* means "Sun Mountain." It is the Aymara name for a mountain in northern Chile. The bands play traditional instruments including the *quena*, a flute of a single reed, and the *zampona*, a panpipe made of reeds bound together with bright wool. In 2007 Inti-Illimani celebrates its fortieth anniversary with a world tour.

In the climate of free expression since the end of military rule, many musicians flourish. In 2000 the Latin rock/pop band La Ley won a Grammy Award for Best Latin Rock/Alternative Album with their album *Uno*. Contemporary singer Jacqueline Fuentes points to Nueva Canción as her main influence. In 2004 she released her album *Amo la Vida* (I Love Life). Young singer Nicole is represented by Maverick Musica, pop star Madonna's Latin music label.

Chileans enjoy several well-established cultural institutions. The capital city of Santiago has three symphony orchestras, and Valparaíso and Concepción have one each. The Municipal Theater in Santiago—a regular stopping place for cultural groups touring the South American continent—is one of Latin America's foremost halls for ballet, opera, and concerts. The nation has contributed its share of performers to the world scene, including the outstanding pianist Claudio Arrau (1903–1991). His many recordings feature the music of Mozart and other classical composers. Luis Olivares Sandoval (b. 1975) has won international acclaim for his opera singing. He tours Chile with the group Three Chilean Tenors.

Viña del Mar hosts a one-week popular song festival every year. A ten-day classical music festival occurs annually in Frutillar, near Puerto Montt. Both festivals take place in summer in February.

Sports and Recreation

Soccer, called *fútbol* (football), is Chile's most popular sport. Fans fill soccer stadiums to capacity for important matches. Soccer players attain the status of national heroes when Chilean teams perform well in international play. Basketball and tennis are also well-attended spectator sports. Tennis player Marcelo Ríos rose to the top position in the world before his retirement in 2004. Chilean tennis players won two gold medals at the 2004 Summer Olympic Games. Some Chileans are avid horse racing fans. The nation as a whole takes pride in its carefully bred horses. They are among the world's finest. The national team usually does well in Olympic equestrian events.

COWBOYS IN CHILE

Chilean cowboys (*below*), called *huasos*, herd cattle in the Central Valley. Their sturdy, smart horses are descendants of Spanish horses. Huasos dress for the elements. Black leather leggings with long fringe protect their legs from thick brush. A poncho, or shoulder cape, keeps them warm. Boots are outfitted with spurs. Wide hats with flat tops—straw in summer and wool felt in winter—complete the outfit. Huasos mostly work alone. They gather for rodeo competitions to show off their riding and cattle-herding skills. The central event is calf pinning. A pair of huasos must herd an untamed young bull twice around a ring and pin it against a marked rail. Rodeo season falls between September and May and provides popular outings for city dwellers.

Two men go **white-water rafting** in Chile. To explore Chile's rafting and other sports adventures, check out the links at www.vgsbooks.com.

Chile's schools have excellent teams in track-and-field events. Bicycle racing is popular, and youngsters often participate in the sport. During the winter, skiers from Chile and abroad flock to the Andean slopes. During the summer, Viña del Mar attracts thousands of people from the Santiago area in search of sea, sun, and sand.

Fishing and hunting interest many Chileans. Along the Pacific Ocean, resorts and local businesses feature fishing contests with prizes for catching marlin and swordfish.

Chile has taken advantage of its beautiful scenery to establish parks in the Andes. In the mountains, the Bío-Bío River is one of the world's best rivers for white-water rafting. Chileans enjoy camping at public parks or private campgrounds located in scenic areas such as the Lake Country.

Food

Chileans generally eat a light breakfast, such as toast with butter and jam. Morning coffee blended with an equal amount of hot milk makes a drink called *café con leche*. The day's main meal is eaten in the early afternoon. Tea and cake or pastries are served in the late afternoon, a social custom adopted from Chile's British immigrants. The last meal of the day is served in the evening between eight and ten.

In low-income homes, beans and rice are common foods, supplemented by cheese and fruit. Meat or fish is occasionally available too. Thick soups of corn or rice, mixed with vegetables and chicken or other meats, are also common.

Among the middle class and the wealthy, the major meal of the day regularly features soup, meat or seafood, and vegetables. Dessert and

CHILEAN SQUASH CASSEROLE

This recipe includes many vegetables native to the Americas. It is hearty enough to serve as a vegetarian main dish. Serve with corn bread and salad.

2 tablespoons olive oil

1 onion, chopped

2 cloves garlic, crushed

1 teaspoon ground cumin

½ teaspoon cayenne (ground red pepper)

1½ cups mixed red and green bell peppers, chopped

2 tomatoes, chopped

½ teaspoon salt

4 eggs, beaten

1 cup cheddar cheese, grated

4 cups butternut squash, cooked and pureed

1 cup corn, fresh or frozen

1. Heat olive oil in frying pan. Turn heat to low, and cook onions, garlic, and spices in oil for 10 minutes.
2. Add peppers, tomatoes, and salt. Cover pan, and cook on low for 10 minutes.
3. Mix beaten eggs with the cheese.
4. Add onion mix to mashed squash, along with corn and egg mix. Stir well.
5. Spread mixture into a buttered 2-quart casserole dish.
6. Bake in preheated 350-degree oven for 30 minutes, covered, and 15 minutes uncovered.

Serves 6 to 8

coffee follow the meal. Shrimp, swordfish, tuna, and conger eel are popular seafood offerings.

Many national dishes combine meat with vegetables. *Cazuela de ave*, for example, mixes chicken, potatoes, corn, rice, onions, and peppers. Everybody eats empanadas—turnovers filled with meat, cheese, onions, or other ingredients. Chilean cuisine is not very spicy.

Many adult Chileans drink locally produced wine with their main meal. Muscatel grapes of the dry Elqui Valley are the basis for *pisco*, Chile's national liquor. Fruit juices and herbal teas called *aguitas* are popular beverages.

THE ECONOMY

The World Bank (a United Nations agency) ranks Chile 32 out of 118 countries for total earnings per person. This places the country fourth in earnings among Latin American countries (after Argentina, Uruguay, and Brazil). Chile's growing economy is based on private ownership. Since 1989, when democracy returned to the country, the Chilean economy has grown nearly 6 percent per year. The income per person has nearly doubled. Poverty has declined drastically. Education, health, housing, and other social services have all improved significantly.

Chile's economy faces two main challenges: diversification and inequality. The economy depends too much on one product—copper. The varying prices of copper on the world market make this an unstable situation. In response, the nation has taken steps to diversify its economy. It has successfully developed new products and markets. The country's wealth, however, is not evenly distributed among its people. The wealthiest 10 percent of the population receive 42 percent of the national income. The poorest 10 percent receive just 1 percent.

The government has made it a priority to reduce poverty and to improve access to health care and education. But the level of poverty remains high. Unemployment hovers at the high rate of 8 percent. The rate of unemployment among people aged 17 to 24 is even higher—about 20 percent. And 20 percent of the population lives below the internationally accepted poverty line of $2 a day.

Service Sector and Tourism

The service sector of the economy produces services rather than goods. It includes jobs in health, education, government, banking, retail trade, tourism, and more. This sector provides Chile with 47 percent of its GDP (gross domestic product, or the total value of all the goods and services produced in one year). Most of Chile's workers—63 percent—have service jobs.

The government has promoted tourism since the 1990s. The country's beautiful scenery and historic sights attract 1.5 million visitors yearly. They bring the country more than $1.3 billion. Argentines make up the largest number of visitors, followed by tourists from Peru and the United States. Chile has an international reputation among skiers. The country's best downhill skiing is to be found in the Andes of the Central Valley. The excellent El Colorado and Farellones ski resorts are in this region. Viña del Mar attracts visitors in the summer months. Chile's wealthy citizens have summer homes there. The area boasts fine hotels and a magnificent city theater. Vacationers picnic, swim, and water-ski at a nearby artificial lake.

THE CHUQUICAMATA MINE

The Chuquicamata mine in Chile's northern Atacama Desert is the largest copper mine in the world. Its open pit is 2.5 miles (4 km) long and 1.2 miles (2 km) wide. The pit reaches a depth of 2,070 feet (631 m).

◉ Industry, Mining, and Manufacturing

Chile's industrial sector, including mining and manufacturing, contributes 47 percent of the nation's GDP. It employs 23 percent of the country's workforce.

Chile's vast mineral resources are the country's chief source of export wealth. They require immense investments of money and advanced technology to be efficient and profitable. Throughout much of Chile's history, international groups—mainly U.S., British, and German companies—provided the money and technology to develop mining. Foreign companies marketed Chile's

Tourists visit the **Chuquicamata copper mine.** Native peoples have known about these copper deposits for centuries.

mineral production in response to global demand. Since Allende nationalized the nation's mining industry, Chile's government owns Codelco, the world's largest copper-producing firm. The country has also opened wide tracts of mineral-rich land to foreign-owned mining operations.

With about one-fifth of the world's known copper reserves, Chile produces more copper than any other country. The market price of copper varies on the world market, however. This variability makes copper an unreliable source of national income. Therefore, Chile has developed other mineral exports. These include gold and silver. Of special importance to Chile is molybdenum. This metal is an ingredient in steel. Chile also exports sizable quantities of lead, zinc, mercury, iron ore, coal, and nitrate.

LABOR UNIONS

Chilean workers, with the backing of political leaders, began to organize themselves into trade unions in the mid-1880s. Since then, these labor organizations have become a vital and influential political force. They represent workers in the mining, oil, textile, railroad, and maritime industries. Unions support the candidates of various political parties after they debate the leading issues of the day. Chilean workers still push for themselves to press for improved employment conditions and for better benefits.

About three-quarters of Chilean manufacturing is concentrated in the cities of Santiago, Valparaíso, and Concepción. The balance is widely scattered throughout the country. Domestically owned Chilean firms supply most of the country's consumer goods, such as soft drinks, clothes, processed foods, tobacco, beer, textiles, wood products, and appliances. Factories also produce paper, cement, chemicals, iron, steel, motor vehicles, and tires. A small computer software and hardware industry is developing too.

Agriculture, Fishing, and Forestry

Long before Chile developed its mineral exports, farming and livestock were the backbone of the nation's economy. For most of Chile's history, a small number of families owned most of the nation's farmland. Only 1.5 percent of landowners owned 70 percent of Chile's land. More than forty-five thousand farms were less than 2.5 acres (1 hectare) in size. Land reforms in the 1960s sought to redistribute the land in a fair way. Under Salvador Allende, agrarian reforms fluctuated. Production declined because farmers were reluctant to invest in property whose future ownership was uncertain. Many Chileans who had farmed for generations abandoned their lands. The government tried to make up for the farming decline by encouraging small-scale farmers to form cooperatives so that they could compete better with larger holdings and agribusinesses.

As a result of the 1973 military coup, land reforms experienced a setback. To raise agricultural production, the junta returned many farms to their previous owners and broke up cooperatives.

Chile's agricultural sector, including fishing and forestry, provides 6 percent of the GDP and employs 14 percent of the nation's workforce. Farming activities—concentrated in the Central Valley—are vital as Chile seeks to diversify its economy. Some farms or agribusinesses encompass more than 250,000 acres (101,000 hectares). Chile's government has eliminated many trade barriers so that the country's farmers can gain wider access to markets in industrialized nations. However, only 6 percent of this mountainous country's land is suitable for farming. The majority of Chile's farms are less than 25 acres (10 hectares). Furthermore, poor farmers use old-fashioned methods to work their land. These methods are inefficient and do not produce as many crops as newer methods. Therefore, Chile imports much of its food.

The Central Valley's level lands produce a wide range of crops, including wheat, corn, barley, rice, and oats. Vegetable harvests include beans, potatoes, tomatoes, pumpkins, sugar beets, and

A farmworker harvests **olives** at an olive oil farm south of Santiago. Efforts are under way to increase agricultural exports such as olive oil.

more. Fruit farmers grow grapes (both wine and table varieties), apples, pears, peaches, and citrus fruits. The export of fruit is an important part of Chilean trade. It supplies summer fruit when it is winter in the Northern Hemisphere. Refrigerated ships transport Chile's fruit to Europe, Japan, and North America. Chile's high-quality wines made from the country's grapes have had international success.

Livestock graze on natural grasslands. They account for about one-third of Chile's agricultural output, including meat, poultry, and dairy products. Cattle raising is concentrated in central Chile. Sheep are raised in the extreme southern portion of the country. Their wool is an important agricultural product.

Chile is one of the world's leaders in the fishing industry. Every year, Chile's fishing fleets haul in about 7 million tons (6.5 million metric tons) of fish. The Pacific offers 220 kinds of edible fish. Anchovies, mackerel, and sardines are among the commercially valuable fish in the Pacific. Much of the haul is processed into fish meal and fish oil for overseas markets. In addition, food-processing plants produce canned fish. Fish farms raise fresh salmon for markets in Europe, Japan, and North America. Export earnings from fishing bring in more than $1.7 billion.

The potential of Chile's forests is also impressive. Forests cover more than 20 percent of the nation's land. More than 1 million acres (405,000 hectares) are planted in pine trees. The plantations exist

Loggers harvest pine trees on a plantation in southern Chile. Forestry has great potential in Chile.

mainly on lands that have been carefully reforested. Loggers harvest the trees for wood, wood products, paper, and cardboard.

Free Trade

Chile's economy is led by exports. Once dependent on copper exports, the country exports thousands of products. Geography long isolated Chileans from the world market. But in modern times, they have access to a full array of consumer goods imported from around the world. Argentina, the United States, Brazil, China, and Germany are Chile's major import suppliers.

Since the 1990s, Chile's democratic government has promoted economic growth by tearing down barriers to foreign trade (such as taxes on imported goods). The state encourages free trade and foreign investment from other nations. In recent years, Chile has signed a number of free-trade agreements with various countries. These include Mexico, the United States, the European Union, and China, as well as many South

Chile's average economic growth rate of 7.7 percent in the 1990s was so high that Chile earned the nickname the Tiger of South America. Its economy is still growing at a respectable rate of 4 to 6 percent.

American countries. The agreements allow for the free flow of goods without restrictions between countries. Chile benefits from high copper prices on the world market, especially in China. Chile also earns income from its exports of fresh fruit, seafood, and forest products. Major export markets are the United States, Japan, Great Britain, China, Brazil, and Mexico.

Energy, Transportation, and Communication

Chile has limited amounts of petroleum and natural gas. Hydropower produces about 50 percent of the country's electricity. Chile imports most of the energy it needs. Its main sources of oil are Argentina and Brazil.

Chile's rough landscape slowed the development of transportation within the country for centuries. Until modern times, ships traveling from port to port were the main transportation system. Railroads in the 1900s replaced ships, except in the far south. Only in the 1990s was a road completed from Puerto Montt to southernmost Chile. Cars and buses provide transportation for most Chileans. Santiago has a subway, which reduces surface traffic in the heavily polluted city. The nation has almost 50,000 miles (80,000 km) of roads, 10,000 miles (16,000 km) of which are paved. Railways connect Chile with its neighbors.

Air travel is still often the best form of transportation to overcome Chile's mountains, deserts, forests, and glaciers. Chile has 364 airports, 74 of them with paved runways. Regular flights link Santiago with Buenos

Many Chileans in cities such as Santiago ride the city bus to get where they need to go.

STUDENTS STRIKE

A generation of young adults has grown up in a democratic Chile. They hold no memories of a life of fear under dictatorship. Many feel free to speak out for greater democracy. On May 30, 2006, about 600,000 high school students and teachers walked out of classes. Some parents supported them. At first, they demanded simple changes, including an end to college-entrance exam fees. Police arrested hundreds of students. After unsatisfactory talks with the government, the students declared a strike. Their demands increased to include better funding of education. The students want a change to the system in which poor children struggle to get an education, while well-off students pay to attend elite private schools. President Bachelet promised a more open government when she took office only a few months before the strike.

Aires, the capital of Argentina. Large passenger planes fly through foggy, 12,674-foot (3,863 m) Uspallata Pass. Above this pass, passengers may look down and see Argentina's huge Christ of the Andes statue.

Chile's telephone system is based on microwave radio relay links and satellite systems. Chileans employ 6.5 million mobile cellular phones and 3.5 million landlines. Internet users number more than 3.5 million. About the same number of homes have television sets, and almost every home has a radio. Chileans access national and local television stations along with cable TV networks, which carry shows from abroad.

Chile was the first country in South America to have a regularly published newspaper. *La Aurora de Chile* (Chile's Dawn) was first printed in 1810. In the twenty-first century, Chile publishes more than seventy daily newspapers. Some are government-owned, but most are private. A 2001 law removed most Pinochet-era restrictions on the media. The constitution guarantees freedom of speech and of the media. Journalists are free to criticize the government and to report on sensitive issues.

⊙ The Future

President Bachelet continues Chile's successful economic model that encourages private enterprise and foreign investment. The government

Visit www.vgsbooks.com for links to websites with additional information about the economy of Chile. See what the exchange rate is from U.S. dollars to Chilean pesos.

is well positioned because, for the first time in years, its coalition party has a majority in the National Congress. Economic growth and diversification are priorities for Chile. The government aims to combine these priorities with policies to achieve social justice, a reduction in poverty, and more equality between the rich and the poor. Programs are in place to improve the health care and educational systems. The government also strives to keep the delicate balance between the country's industries and environmental protection.

Chile has come far from the tragedies of the Allende and Pinochet eras. A flourishing democracy with a sound economy is well established. The nation enjoys a free press and full civil rights. Chileans look with hope toward the future.

THE LEAST CORRUPT NATION IN LATIN AMERICA

Chile ranks 21 out of 159 in the world in a survey of countries with the least corruption in business and government. Transparency International, an anticorruption organization, conducted the survey. In its yearly index, the organization ranked Chile 7.4 out of 10. This ranking makes Chile the least corrupt nation in Latin America.

Timeline

CA. 10,000 B.C. The first people settle in the area of present-day Chile. Native peoples live by farming corn, beans, and potatoes and by fishing and hunting.

A.D. 1400S The Inca civilization of Peru conquers Chile's Mapuche people in the north. The Mapuche retreat to the south.

1520 Portuguese explorer Ferdinand Magellan finds what is later called the Strait of Magellan when winds blow his ships off course.

1540 Spaniard Pedro de Valdivia and his men enter Mapuche territory after a difficult march through the Andes. The Mapuche resist the Spaniards.

1541 Valdivia and his troops establish Chile's first Spanish settlement at Santiago. Chile becomes a colony of Spain.

1560S Spanish soldier-poet Alonso de Ercilla y Zúñiga writes *La Araucana*.

1810 On September 18, Chile's ruling landowners declare Chile's independence from Spain at a town meeting.

1811 Chile's first National Congress meets. Bernardo O'Higgins Riquelme—Chile's Father of Independence—is among the lawmakers.

1818 Chile gains full independence from Spain on February 12.

1843 The University of Chile is founded.

1851 Manuel Montt becomes Chile's first nonmilitary president. During his administration, large numbers of German immigrants arrive in Chile.

1879 Chile's disagreements with Bolivia and Peru over land boundaries erupt into the five-year War of the Pacific.

1883 Chile defeats Bolivia and Peru and wins ownership of its mineral-rich northern region. The Mapuche are moved onto reservations.

1891 Civil war erupts over a constitutional dispute between President Balmaceda and the National Congress. Defeat of Balmaceda leads to greater congressional power.

1907 Government troops kill two thousand workers striking in Iquique.

1927 General Carlos Ibáñez del Campo becomes president and establishes a dictatorship.

1935 Women in Chile win the right to vote.

1945 Poet Gabriela Mistral wins the Nobel Prize for Literature.

1948 For the next ten years, the Communist Party is banned. Communists—including Pablo Neruda—are purged from the government.

1960 An earthquake on May 22 on Chile's coast registers 8.6 on the Richter scale, kills one thousand people, and causes millions of dollars in damage.

1964 Eduardo Frei Montalva becomes president. He introduces some social reforms but fails to curb inflation.

1970 Salvador Allende becomes the first democratically elected Marxist president in the Western Hemisphere. He begins to nationalize Chile's industries, especially copper.

1971 Pablo Neruda becomes Chile's second Nobel Prize-winning poet.

1973 General Pinochet overthrows President Allende in a CIA-sponsored coup. He leads a military junta in brutally cracking down on people who supported Allende or oppose his dictatorship. Thousands are killed, tortured, or exiled under Pinochet's rule.

1975 The Catholic Church's prisoner relief agency counts 750 disappearances in this year alone. Most of those who disappeared were murdered by the military.

1988 Chileans vote against Pinochet remaining in power.

1989 Patricio Aylwin is elected Chile's first democratic president since Salvador Allende.

1990 Pinochet ends his rule as president but remains commander in chief of the army. During the 1990s, Chile's economic growth rate of 7.7 percent earns the country the nickname the Tiger of South America.

1993 Eduardo Frei wins the presidential election.

1998 Pinochet retires from the army, but he becomes a senator for life. He is arrested in Great Britain at the request of Spain.

2000 Ricardo Lagos is elected president. Pinochet returns to Chile. La Ley wins a Grammy Award for Best Latin Rock/Alternative album with their album, *Uno*

2002 Chile's Supreme Court rules that Pinochet is unfit to stand trial. Pinochet resigns from his post as a lifelong senator. Environmental activists protest against mining, logging, and a proposed dam on the Bío-Bío River. Mapuche activists demand the return of native lands.

2003 Courts block attempts to force Pinochet to stand trial and to lift his legal immunity.

2004 Manuel Contreras, former head of the secret police, is found guilty of the 1974 death of a journalist. President Lagos defies the Catholic Church and signs a law giving Chileans the right to divorce.

2006 Voters elect the country's first woman president—Michelle Bachelet Jeria. She is the fourth president in a row from the center-left Concertación coalition. Despite economic improvements, 20 percent of Chile's population lives on less than $2 a day. Chile ranks as the least corrupt nation in Latin America.

COUNTRY NAME Republic of Chile

AREA 292,135 square miles (756,630 sq. km)

MAIN LANDFORMS Andes Mountains, the Archipelago, Atacama Desert, Central Valley, Easter Island, Pacific Coast, Tierra del Fuego, Valdivian Coastal Range

HIGHEST POINT Ojos del Salado, 22,572 feet (6,880 m) above sea level

MAJOR RIVERS Bío-Bío, Copiapó, Elqui, Huasco, Itata, Loa, Maipo, Mapocho, Maule

ANIMALS Alpacas, albatrosses, anchovies, Andean wolves, chinchillas, condors, cormorants, flamingos, guanacos, guemuls, Humboldt penguins, hummingbirds, jaguars, llamas, Magellanic penguins, marsupials, mountain monkeys, otters, parrots, pelicans, pumas, salmon, sea lions, seals, spike-horned pudus, storm petrel, tuna, vicuñas

CAPITAL CITY Santiago

OTHER MAJOR CITIES Antofagasta, Arica, Concepción, Iquique, Temuco, Valparaíso, Viña del Mar

OFFICIAL LANGUAGE Spanish

MONETARY UNITY Chilean peso (CLP). 1 peso = 100 centavos

Fast Facts

Currency

CURRENCY

The peso has been Chile's national currency since 1975. Peso coins are available in denominations of 1, 5, 10, 50, and 100. The coins carry an image of Chile's national coat of arms. Bills (paper money) come in denominations of 500, 1,000, 2,000, 5,000, and 10,000 pesos. Pictures of Chile's famous people appear on the bills. Nobel laureate Gabriela Mistral is on the 5,000-peso bill.

Chile's flag is red, white, and blue. It has a band of white at the top and an equal-sized band of red below. A blue square the same height as the white band sits at the left side of the white band. Inside the blue square is a white five-pointed star. The star is a symbol of pride and progress. Blue stands for the sky. White represents the snow-covered Andes. Red symbolizes the blood spilled to win Chile's independence from Spain.

The Himno Nacional de Chile (National Anthem of Chile) is commonly known as the Canción Nacional (National Song). Ramón Carnicer y Battle wrote the music, adopted in 1828. The young poet Eusebio Lillo Robles wrote the lyrics, adopted in 1847. The song contains seven verses plus the chorus. But only the fifth verse and the chorus make up the official national anthem. Below is the chorus.

English Chorus:
Gentle homeland, accept the vows
Given, Chile, on your altars,
That you be either the tomb of the free
Or a refuge from oppression.

Spanish Chorus:
Dulce Patria, recibe los votos
Con que Chile en tus aras juró
Que o la tumba serás de los libres
O el asilo contra la opresión

For a link where you can listen to Chile's national anthem, go to www.vgsbooks.com.

SALVADOR ALLENDE (1908–1973) Allende became Chile's president in 1970. He was born in Valparaíso and studied medicine at the University of Chile. A founder of Chile's Socialist Party, he served in the National Congress starting in 1937. As the minister of health, Allende worked to improve the lives of workers and the poor. As president, he announced, "The riches of Chile are enormous. We will fight to recover them." And he quickly took Chile's copper industry away from foreign owners. This was popular in Chile but won him enemies in the United States. On September 11, 1973, the army overthrew him, and Allende committed suicide. He did not receive a formal burial until 1990. Allende and his wife, Hortensia Bussi, had three daughters.

DANIELA ANGUITA (b. 1984) Anguita is a downhill ski racer. She represented Chile in alpine skiing at the 2006 Winter Olympics. She was the flag bearer at the opening ceremonies. Born in Spain, she attends college at the University of Alaska.

CLAUDIO ARRAU (1903–1991) Arrau, born in Chillán, was a Chilean pianist and teacher. When Arrau was eight, the Chilean government sent him to Berlin, Germany, to study piano. He played and recorded widely, performing works by Mozart and Schubert. He was well known for the creativity and skill of his playing.

MICHELLE BACHELET JERIA (b. 1951) Born in Santiago, Michelle Bachelet was sworn in as Chile's first woman president on March 11, 2006. As a young woman, she worked secretly for a group that opposed Pinochet. The military arrested her but in 1975 allowed her to leave the country. She studied medicine in Germany. When she returned to Chile, she served in the government as health minister and defense minister. Bachelet is separated from her husband and has three children.

ROBERTO MATTA (1911–2002) Chile's most famous painter, Roberto Antonio Sebastián Matta Echaurren was born in Santiago. He studied architecture and interior design in college. In 1933 he moved to Europe for life. Painters Salvador Dali and Pablo Picasso influenced his art. Matta's paintings explore dreams and the subconscious and focus on the spiritual and social destruction of war and machines. He used luminous colors including deep crimson, yellow, blue, and black.

GABRIELA MISTRAL (1889–1957) In 1945 Mistral became the first Latin American to win the Nobel Prize for Literature. In her acceptance speech, she said: "I am the direct voice of the poets of my race and the indirect voice for the noble Spanish and Portuguese tongues. Both rejoice to have been invited to this festival of . . . life. . . ." Mistral was born Lucila Godoy Alcayaga in the village of Vicuña. She worked as a teacher and diplomat. Mistral's simple, direct poems are full of warmth and emotion. Her themes include love, pain, and recovery.

PABLO NERUDA (1904–1973) Known as the people's poet, Neruda was born Naftali Ricardo Reyes Basoalto in the village of Parral. When he was twenty, his first book of poems brought him huge success. Neruda served Chile as a diplomat. But he came into conflict with the government after he joined the Communist Party, and he lived in exile until 1952. Neruda's poetry celebrates love, nature, and ordinary things, such as socks. His series of poems *Canto General* (1950) captures the struggles of the Chilean people. In his *Memoirs*, he said of his life, "I had to suffer and struggle, to love and sing; I drew my worldly share of triumphs and defeats, I tasted bread and blood. What more can a poet want?" Neruda was married three times and had one daughter, Malva Marina.

VIOLETA DEL CARMEN PARRA SANDOVAL (1917–1967) Parra, one of Chile's most famous musicians, was born in San Carlos. Parra was instrumental in the Chilean folk music movement. Its influence reached far beyond Chile. Active in politics, Parra also was a noted visual artist. Part of a talented family, she performed widely with her son, Angel, and daughter, Isabel. Her brother, Nicanor Parra, is a modern poet. Parra took her own life at the age of fifty, over an unhappy love affair. Her song, "Gracias a la Vida," remains one of the most performed songs from Latin America.

AUGUSTO PINOCHET UGARTE (b. 1915) Pinochet was the head of the military junta that ruled Chile from 1973 to 1990. He was born in Valparaíso. President Allende made him commander in chief of the army. In September 1973, General Pinochet led the coup against Allende. He gave orders that led to thousands of Chileans being killed, tortured, or forced out of the country. In 1974 Pinochet appointed himself president and ruled as a dictator. To his surprise, he lost the 1988 vote to continue his rule. He has been fighting legal battles for years, including charges of illegal bank accounts. Pinochet remains under house arrest.

MARCELO ANDRÉS RÍOS MAYORGA (b. 1975) Born in Santiago, Ríos ranked as the world's number one junior tennis player at seventeen. In 1998 he rose to the world's number one singles ranking—the first male player from Latin America to do so. He retired in 2004, but in 2006 he won an exclusive senior championship. Ríos married twice and has one daughter, Constanza, born in 2001.

IVÁN LUIS ZAMORANO ZAMORA (b. 1967) Zamorano, born in Santiago, is a Chilean soccer idol. His nicknames are Bam Bam (from *The Flintstones*) and Ivan the Terrible. He played for Chile sixty-nine times and scored thirty-four goals. In the 2000 Summer Olympic Games, he was the top scorer and won the bronze medal. Zamorano retired in 2003 and is a goodwill ambassador for UNICEF (United Nations Children's Fund). He and his Argentine model wife, María Alberó, had their first child in 2006.

LAKE COUNTRY This region from Temuco to Puerto Montt is one of South America's main tourist destinations. Its beautiful scenery includes snowcapped volcanoes, deep blue lakes, rain forests, and rivers with rapids. Many national parks in the district offer river rafting, hiking trails, and ski and snowboard slopes.

LAUCA NATIONAL PARK Lauca is northern Chile's treasure, located east of Arica. Landmarks here trace the history of pre-Spanish peoples. More than one hundred kinds of birds, including flamingos, flock here. It is also home to alpacas and vizcachas, animals related to the chinchilla. The park's Lake Chungará is one of the world's highest lakes. It sits at the foot of dormant twin volcanoes.

RAPA NUI NATIONAL PARK Rapa Nui is the native name for Easter Island. The national park is a UNESCO (a United Nations agency) site. It covers most of the island's coastline and protects the multiton sculptures of volcanic rock. Looming up to 20 feet (6 m) tall, the statues might represent chiefs and gods.

SANTIAGO Chile's capital city offers museums, parks, and markets where artisans make and sell their crafts. The unique Mirador Interactive Museum has mechanical toys you can climb on, a bed of nails you can lie on, and other hands-on exhibits. The Pre-Columbian Art Museum's collection includes blowguns and darts. You can see Chilean mummies, a giant whale, and artifacts from Easter Island at the Natural History Museum. Visitors can take horseback or hiking expeditions into the nearby Andes Mountains.

TORRES DEL PAINE NATIONAL PARK Located in the far south, this is Chile's most famous national park. *Torres* is Spanish for "towers"—the shape of the ice-capped mountains in the park. A ten-day hiking trail is the best way to see the rugged landscape and spectacular wildlife. No cars are allowed in the park, but visitors can rent packhorses.

VALLE DEL ENCANTO ARCHAEOLOGICAL MUSEUM The museum is located in the north, near San Pedro de Atacama. Nearby, the Río Limarí canyon contains impressive rock art from the area's native culture about A.D. 600. This is a popular spot for picnics or camping.

VALPARAÍSO AREA Valparaíso's historic seaport area is another UNESCO site. The Maritime Museum displays Chile's oceangoing history. The city's cable railway goes up into the colorful hillside neighborhoods. It is a short bus ride to the beach resort of Viña del Mar. Visitors can rent horses to ride along the beach, and penguins might be visible on offshore islands. A longer bus ride takes you to Isla Negra—a rocky headland on the sea where Neruda lived and is buried.

Araucanian: the name the Spanish used for all the native people of Chile. The Mapuche are the country's largest indigenous group.

capitalism: a system of private ownership. The economies of Chile and the United States are based on capitalism.

coalition: a union made up of different parties and groups. Chile's Concertación coalition has led Chile's government since 1990.

Communism: a political and economic theory that proposes no private ownership. Its goal is to create economic equality. In a wholly Communist society, all goods would be owned in common.

dictator: a leader who rules with complete control, often through the use of harsh methods

free trade: exchange of goods between nations, with no restrictions. Free trade agreements remove protective tariffs (taxes that make imported goods more expensive).

glacier: a slow-moving mass of ice. Glaciers exist in Chile's cold far south.

gross domestic product (GDP): the value of the goods and services produced by a country over a period of time, usually one year

junta: a group that controls a government, especially one that has violently taken power

land reform: measures a government takes to redistribute farmland in a more fair way

Latin America: Mexico, Central America, South America, and the islands of the West Indies. Latin America includes thirty-three independent countries and thirteen other political units.

literacy: the ability to read and write a basic sentence

magic realism: a literary style that became popular in Latin America in the 1970s. Magic realism blends dreams and imagination with everyday reality.

mestizo: a person with mixed native and Spanish ancestry. Most Chileans are mestizos.

moai: large, humanlike statues on Easter Island (Rapa Nui), carved from volcanic rock

rain forest: a dense woodland that receives a large amount of rain. Chile's temperate rain forest has a moderate climate and many kinds of trees compared to a tropical rain forest.

Socialism: a variety of social systems in which the government controls some part of the production and distribution of goods

tectonic plate: a slow-moving plate that forms Earth's crust. The grinding actions of the plates can cause earthquakes and volcanic eruptions.

BBC News. 2006.
http://www.bbc.co.uk **(April 5, 2006).**
The World Edition of the BBC (British Broadcasting Company) News is updated throughout the day, every day. The BBC is a source for comprehensive news coverage about Chile. It also provides a country profile at http://news.bbc.co.uk/go/pr/fr/-/1/hi/world/americas/country_profiles/1222905.stm.

Bizzarro, Salvatore. *Historical Dictionary of Chile*. Lanham, MD: Scarecrow Press, 1987.
A very useful reference book, this dictionary offers short articles on Chile's culture, economics, history, politics, and social issues, as well as informative entries on people, places, and events. Maps and a bibliography are included.

Boinod, Adam Jacot de. *The Meaning of Tingo*. New York: Penguin Press, 2006.
Words from Pascuense, a language spoken on Chile's Easter Island, are included in this amusing book of words from around the world.

Buckman, Robert T. *Latin America 2005*. Harpers Ferry, WV: Stryker-Post Publications, 2005.
Part of the annual World Today series, this publication includes a long article on Chile. It presents an overview of Chile's history, government, culture, and economy.

Central Intelligence Agency (CIA). "Chile." *The World Factbook*. 2006.
http://www.cia.gov/cia/publications/factbook/geos/ci.html **(March 29, 2006).**
This CIA website provides facts and figures on Chile's geography, people, government, economy, communications, transportation, military, and more.

Cooper, Marc. *Pinochet and Me: A Chilean Anti-Memoir*. London and New York: Verso, 2001.
The author, an American journalist, was President Allende's translator until the 1973 coup. In this book, Cooper relates his experiences and feelings in the days leading up to and immediately after the coup, including listening to the live broadcast of Allende's last words.

Energy Information Administration. *Country Analysis Brief: Chile*. September 2005.
http://www.eia.doe.gov/emeu/cabs/Chile/Background.html **(March 2006).**
This site is one of the most complete sources of energy statistics on the Internet. It offers information about energy production and use in Chile and other countries of the world. The site also includes Web links and a kids' section about energy.

Hubbard, Carolyn, Brigitte Barta, and Jeff Davis. *Chile and Easter Island*. Footscray, AUS: Lonely Planet, 2003.
More than a guidebook, this Lonely Planet publication offers an overview of Chile's history, geography, environment, language, and culture. Maps, color photographs, drawings, a glossary, and reading suggestions also accompany useful travel information. Lonely Planet's website about Chile can be found at http://www.lonelyplanet.com/worldguide/destinations/south-america/chile-and-easter-island/.

Library of Congress, Federal Research Division. *A Country Study: Chile.* 1994.
http://lcweb2.loc.gov/frd/cs/cltoc.html (January 2006).
This country study prepared by the U.S. Federal Research Division covers the main historical, social, economic, political, and national security aspects of Chile. Sources of information include scholarly publications, official reports and documents of government and international organizations, and foreign and domestic newspapers and periodicals.

Neruda, Pablo. *The Poetry of Pablo Neruda.* Edited and with an introduction by Ilan Stavans. New York: Farrar, Straus and Giroux, 2003.
This selection presents more than six hundred of Neruda's poems. Titles reflect the poet's wide-ranging subject matter, from "Love" to "Revolutions" to "Ode to a Pair of Socks."

Population Reference Bureau. 2005.
http://www.prb.org (March 2006).
PRB provides annual, in-depth demographics on Chile's population. It includes rates of birth, death, and infant mortality and other statistics relating to health, environment, education, employment, family planning, and more. Special articles cover environmental and health issues.

Roraff, Susan, and Laura Camacho. *Culture Shock! Chile.* Portland, OR: Graphic Arts Center Publishing, 1998.
This book is a guide to customs and etiquette, designed for foreigners living in Chile. It offers information on food, language, religion, social behavior, business practices, and more.

South America, *Central America and the Caribbean 2006.* London: Routledge, 2005.
The long section on Chile in this annual publication covers the country's recent history, geography, and culture. It also provides a detailed look at the economy, politics, and government of the nation. Statistics and sources are included too. This is a volume in the Europa Regional Surveys of the World series.

U.S. Department of State, Bureau of Western Hemisphere Affairs. *Background Note: Chile.* March 2006.
http://www.state.gov/r/pa/ei/bgn/1981.htm (April 5, 2006).
The background notes of the U.S. State Department supplies a profile of Chile's people, history, government, political conditions, and economy. The State Department also provides travel information for Americans going abroad.

Allende, Isabel. *My Invented Country: A Nostalgic Journey through Chile.* **Translated by Margaret Sayers Peden. New York: HarperCollins, 2003.**
Allende is the author of seven novels, many short stories, and a trilogy of children's books. This memoir is a portrait of the geography, history, and personality of her native land.

Allende Gossens, Salvador. "Salvador Allende's Last Speech (English Translation)." **Translated by Joe Mabel.** *Wikipedia.*
http://en.wikisource.org/wiki/Salvador_Allende%27s_Last_Speech_%28English_translation%29.
Read the complete text of President Allende's live radio broadcast on September 11, 1973, shortly before his death.

Arnold, Caroline. *Easter Island: Giant Stone Statues Tell of a Rich and Tragic Past.* **New York: Clarion Books, 2000.**
The author is also a photographer, and this book for younger readers is full of fascinating photographs of Easter Island's mysterious stone figures in their dramatic landscape. The text explains the people, their legends, and daily life.

Brown, Monica. *My Name Is Gabriela: The Life of Gabriela Mistral.* **Flagstaff, AZ: Luna Rising, 2005.**
Charming illustrations accompany this book for young readers. It follows the life of the Chilean Nobel Prize-winning poet from her childhood, when she taught herself to read, through her lifelong love of words.

Del Rio, Ana Maria. *Carmen's Rust.* **New York: Overlook, 2003.**
This novel for young adults tells the grim story of a teenage girl named Carmen. She lives with uptight relatives in Santiago, Chile. When Carmen falls in love, her aunt banishes her to an isolated room. The novel, written during the Pinochet era, presents the way Carmen becomes the victim of her unfair family, the way many Chileans fell victim to an unfair government.

Embassy of Chile, Washington D.C.
http://www.chile-usa.org
Chile's embassy is located in Washington, D.C. Its site offers links and information on Chile's culture, politics, land, travel, and more.

Garza, Hedda. *Salvador Allende.* **New York: Chelsea House, 1989.**
Part of the World Leaders series, this biography for young adults presents the life of Chile's Socialist president. It also tells the story of how the Chilean military overthrew Allende's government.

Goodnough, David. *Pablo Neruda: Nobel Prize-Winning Poet.* **Berkeley Heights, NJ: Enslow Publishers, 1998.**
A biography of the great Chilean poet, this book is part of the Hispanic Biographies series for younger readers. It traces Neruda's life from his youthful romantic poetry to his life in exile and his 1971 Nobel Prize for Literature.

Further Reading and Websites

Heyerdahl, Thor. *Aku-Aku: The Secret of Easter Island*. **New York: Pocket Books, 1977.**
This book is an account of the author's expedition to Easter Island in 1955–1956. Heyerdahl explores the mysteries of the island's stone statues. The local people demonstrate that they still know how to transport and lift up the heavy stone statues.

Lourie, Peter. *Tierra del Fuego*. **Honesdale, PA: Boyds Mills Press, 2002.**
History, adventure, and both new and old maps are matched with amazing photographs of this land at the end of South America.

Mapuche International Link
http://www.mapuche-nation.org/
This website aims to highlight the current situation of the Mapuche people. It presents their culture, history, and hopes for the future.

Maynard, Charles W. *The Andes*. **New York: Rosen Publishing, 2004.**
This book is part of the Great Mountain Ranges of the World series for younger readers. It looks at the geology and biology of the Andes.

McNair, Sylvia. *Chile*. **New York: Children's Press, 2000.**
Part of the Enchantment of the World series for younger readers, this volume describe the history, geography, economy, and culture of Chile.

Parnell, Helga. *Cooking the South American Way*. **Minneapolis: Lerner Publications Company, 2003.**
Focusing on recipes from countries including Argentina, Brazil, and Chile, this cookbook offers a sampling of tastes from across the continent.

Selby, Anna. *Argentina, Chile, Paraguay, Uruguay*. **Austin, TX: Raintree Steck-Vaughn, 1999.**
Chile shares the southern triangle of South America with Argentina, Paraguay, and Uruguay. This book is part of the Country Fact Files series for younger readers. It compares the history, geography, and societies of the four countries.

Travel for Kids
http://www.travelforkids.com/Funtodo/Chile/chile.htm
This site asks, "Chile—where else can kids ski on July 4th, go swimming at the beach on Christmas, watch condors soaring on the currents, eat German pastries, and set foot on Tierra del Fuego?"

vgsbooks.com
http://www.vgsbooks.com
Visit vgsbooks.com, the home page of the Visual Geography Series®, which is updated regularly. You can get linked to all sorts of useful online information, including geographical, historical, demographic, cultural, and economic websites. The vgsbooks.com site is a great resource for late-breaking news and statistics.

Winter, Jane Kohen, and Susan Roraff. *Chile*. **New York: Marshall Cavendish, 2002.**
This title in the Cultures of the World series for younger readers offers an introduction to the history, geography, culture, and lifestyles of Chile. Photos, charts, and maps add to the informational text.

Aconcagua River, 9, 10
Aguirre Cerda, Pedro, 28
Allende Gossens, Salvador, 5–7, 28, 29–31, 50, 51, 59, 70, 71
alpaca, 15, 68
Andes, 4, 8, 12–13, 14, 21, 39, 43, 54, 58, 68
Argentina, 8, 12, 13, 38, 58, 64
arts and crafts, 48
Atacama Desert, 9, 10, 68
Aylwin Azócar, Patricio, 33, 34

Bachelet Jeria, Michelle, 7, 35–36, 64, 70
Bolivia, 5, 8, 38, 40

Cape Horn, 12, 13
capitalism, 5, 7
Chile: environmental threats to, 16, 35, 65; flag of 69; history of, 20–35; and independence from Spain, 4, 23–34; landscape and boundaries, 4, 8–10; map of, 6, 11; military government of, 7, 25, 27, 29, 31–34, 46, 51; mineral wealth of, 5, 10, 15, 18, 25, 26, 29, 56, 58–59; national anthem of, 69; natural resources of, 7, 15–17, 26, 27, 28; 1973 coup in, 7, 31, 36, 51, 60, 70, 71; population of, 17, 38–41, 44; as a Spanish colony, 4, 21, 22–23
Chilean Antarctic Territory, 8
cities, 17–19, 44–45
climate, 13–14
Concepción, 10, 19, 52, 68
culture, 19, 43, 46–52

Easter Island, 9, 41, 68, 72
economy, 5, 27, 32–33, 56–63; growth of, 7, 25, 26, 32, 33, 34, 56, 62, 65. See also capitalism
education, 5, 25, 26, 34, 41–42, 56, 64, 65
environmental threats, 16, 35, 65

farming and cattle raising, 10, 13, 15, 18, 20, 22, 23, 32, 53, 59–61
fishing, 16, 18, 20, 54, 60, 61
flora and fauna, 14–15
food, 54–55

glaciers, 10, 12, 63
government, 16, 23, 24, 27–31; Communist, 30, 32; democratic, 7, 26, 29, 32, 33, 56, 64, 65
guanaco, 15

health, 43, 56, 57, 65
holidays and festivals, 48, 53
human rights abuse, 7, 19, 21, 32, 34, 35, 71
hydroelectric power, 13, 15, 63

Incas, 15, 20, 21
industry, 58–59, 65

labor issues, 26, 28, 30–31, 33, 44, 57, 59
Lake Country, 10, 14, 72
language, 42
Lautaro, 22
literature, 49–50
living conditions, 17, 26, 44

Magellan, Ferdinand, 21
maps, 6, 11
Mapuche, 18, 20–21, 22, 35, 40, 48; resistance by, 22, 40
Matta, Roberto, 48, 70
mestizos, 22, 38–39
mining, 25, 26, 29, 45, 58–59
Montt, Manuel, 25
movies and film, 49, 50–51
music, 51–53

national parks, 16, 54, 72
native peoples, 4, 20–22, 23, 39–41, 47, 48, 52. See also Mapuche
natural disasters, 16–17, 18, 29
Neruda, Pablo, 28, 29, 49, 71

O'Higgins Riquelme, Bernardo, 23–24
oil, 12, 15–16, 59
ozone layer, 16

Pacific Ocean, 4, 8, 13, 16, 54
Peru, 5, 8, 9, 20, 38, 40, 52

Pinochet Ugarte, Augusto, 7, 31, 32, 33, 70, 71; arrest of, 7, 34; trial of, 7, 37
Pizarro, Francisco, 21
Puerto Montt, 10, 12, 14, 40, 53
Punta Arenas, 12, 16, 19

recipe, 55
religion, 46–48; Catholicism, 24; freedom of, 27, 46. *See also* Roman Catholic Church
Ring of Fire, 16
Robinson Crusoe Island, 9
Roman Catholic Church, 4, 22–23, 24, 25, 26, 27, 32, 35, 41, 47

Santiago, 4, 10, 13, 14, 16, 17–18, 23, 37, 39, 43, 44, 47, 52, 63, 68, 72
sheep raising, 12, 15, 44, 31
slavery, 22, 23

slums. *See* living conditions
sports, 53–54
Strait of Magellan, 12, 13, 19

Tierra del Fuego, 12, 68
tourism, 57–58
transportation, 5, 18, 23, 63–64

unemployment, 32, 57
United States, 29, 58, 62, 70. *See also* U.S. Central Intelligence Agency (CIA)
U.S. Central Intelligence Agency (CIA), 7, 30–31

vicuña, 10, 15

War of the Pacific, 4–5, 26
World War II, 5

Captions for photos appearing on cover and chapter openers:

Cover: A waterfall in southern Chile

pp. 4–5 Sheep graze on a plain beneath the snowcapped Andes Mountains.

pp. 8–9 The city of Puerto Montt lies on the Gulf of Reloncavi. The Tronador Volcano is in the distance.

pp. 20–21 These giant statues, called moai, are found on Easter Island. Many theories exist as to why the moai were carved, the most popular one being that each statue represents an ancestor. There are approximately six hundred moai on Easter Island, some of which stand 40 feet (12 m) tall.

pp. 38–39 Four boys in school uniforms pose for a picture in Valparaíso.

pp. 46–47 An artists' fair in Santiago brings out painters and buyers.

pp. 56–57 A worker in the foundry of the Chuquicamata copper mine oversees the process of melting copper.

Photo Acknowledgments
The images in this book are used with the permission of: © John Kreul/Independent Picture Service, pp. 4–5, 12, 15, 20–21, 62; © XNR Productions, pp. 6, 11; © Robin Smith/Art Directors, pp. 8–9; © Chris Rennie/Art Directors, p. 10; © Galen Rowell/CORBIS, p. 14; © Samuel Lund, pp. 17, 18, 38–39, 41, 44, 45; © Kean Collection/Getty Images, p. 23; © Bettmann/CORBIS, p. 25; © Keystone/Getty Images, p. 29 (top); © AFP/Getty Images, pp. 29 (bottom), 30; © Julio Etchart/Impact Photos/ZUMA Press, p. 33; © Gerry Penny/AFP/Getty Images, p. 34; © J.C./Action Press/ZUMA Press, p. 36; © Sam Lund/Independent Picture Service, pp. 40, 42, 46–47, 63; © Bb Holdings Bv/Art Directors, p. 48; © Getty Images, p. 51; © Holton Collection/SuperStock, p. 52; © Ernest Manewal/SuperStock, p. 53; © age fotostock/SuperStock, p. 54; © Martin Bernetti/AFP/Getty Images, pp. 56–57, 58, 60, 61; © Todd Strand/Independent Picture Service, p. 68; © Laura Westlund/Independent Picture Service, p. 69.

Front Cover: © John Kreul/Independent Picture Service.
Back Cover: NASA